THE PRODIGAL GOD

THE
PRODIGAL
GOD

*Recovering the Heart
of the Christian Faith*

TIMOTHY KELLER

DUTTON

DUTTON
Published by Penguin Group (USA) Inc.
375 Hudson Street, New York, New York 10014, U.S.A.
Penguin Group (Canada), 90 Eglinton Avenue East, Suite 700, Toronto,
Ontario M4P 2Y3, Canada (a division of Pearson Penguin Canada Inc.); Penguin
Books Ltd, 80 Strand, London WC2R 0RL, England; Penguin Ireland, 25 St
Stephen's Green, Dublin 2, Ireland (a division of Penguin Books Ltd); Penguin
Group (Australia), 250 Camberwell Road, Camberwell, Victoria 3124, Australia
(a division of Pearson Australia Group Pty Ltd); Penguin Books India Pvt Ltd,
11 Community Centre, Panchsheel Park, New Delhi—110 017, India; Penguin
Group (NZ), 67 Apollo Drive, Rosedale, North Shore 0632, New Zealand (a
division of Pearson New Zealand Ltd); Penguin Books (South Africa) (Pty) Ltd,
24 Sturdee Avenue, Rosebank, Johannesburg 2196, South Africa

Penguin Books Ltd, Registered Offices: 80 Strand, London WC2R 0RL, England

Published by Dutton, a member of Penguin Group (USA) Inc.

First printing, November 2008
3   5   7   9   10   8   6   4

 REGISTERED TRADEMARK—MARCA REGISTRADA

LIBRARY OF CONGRESS CATALOGING-IN-PUBLICATION DATA

Keller, Timothy J., 1950–
The prodigal God: recovering the heart of the Christian faith / by Timothy
Keller.—1st ed.
p.   cm.
ISBN 978-0-525-95079-0 (hardcover)
Special Markets Edition / NOT FOR RESALE
PP ISBN 978-0-525-95148-3
1. Prodigal son (Parable) 2. Christianity. I. Title.
ET378.P8K45 2008
226.8'06—dc22   2008028397

Printed in the United States of America
Set in ITC Galliard
Designed by Leonard Telesca

While the author has made every effort to provide accurate telephone numbers and
Internet addresses at the time of publication, neither the publisher nor the author
assumes any responsibility for errors, or for changes that occur after publication.
Further, the publisher does not have any control over and does not assume any
responsibility for author or third-party Web sites or their content.

WITH GRATITUDE TO
EDMUND P. CLOWNEY
and my other mentors

CONTENTS

Contents

Contents

INTRODUCTION

THIS short book is meant to lay out the essentials of the Christian message, the gospel. It can, therefore, serve as an introduction to the Christian faith for those who are unfamiliar with its teachings or who may have been away from them for some time.

This volume is not just for seekers, however. Many lifelong Christian believers feel they understand the basics of the Christian faith quite well and don't think they need a primer. Nevertheless, one of the signs that you may not grasp the unique, radical nature of the gospel is that you are certain that you do. Sometimes longtime church members find themselves so struck and turned around by a fresh apprehension of the Christian message that they feel themselves to have

been essentially "re-converted." This book, then, is written to both curious outsiders and established insiders of the faith, both to those Jesus calls "younger brothers" and those he calls "elder brothers" in the famous Parable of the Prodigal Son.

I am turning to this familiar story, found in the fifteenth chapter of the gospel of St. Luke, in order to get to the heart of the Christian faith. The parable's plot and *dramatis personae* are very simple. There was a father who had two sons. The younger asked for his share of the inheritance, received it, and promptly left for a far country, where he squandered it all on sensual and frivolous pleasure. He returned home penitently and, to his surprise, was received with open arms by his father. This reception alienated and angered the elder brother greatly. The story closes with the father appealing to his firstborn son to join in the welcome and forgiveness of his younger brother.

On the surface of it, the narrative is not all that gripping. I believe, however, that if the teaching of Jesus is likened to a lake, this famous Parable of the

Introduction

Prodigal Son would be one of the clearest spots where we can see all the way to the bottom. Many excellent studies have been written on this Biblical text over the last several years, but the foundation for my understanding of it was a sermon I first heard preached over thirty years ago by Dr. Edmund P. Clowney. Listening to that sermon changed the way I understood Christianity.[1] I almost felt I had discovered the secret heart of Christianity. Over the years I have often returned to teach and counsel from the parable. I have seen more people encouraged, enlightened, and helped by this passage, when I explained the true meaning of it, than by any other text.[2]

I once traveled overseas and delivered this sermon to an audience through an interpreter. Some time later the translator wrote to tell me that, as he was preaching the sermon, he had realized that the parable was like an arrow aimed at his heart. After a period of wrestling and reflection, it brought him to faith in Christ. Many others have told me that this story of Jesus, once they came to understand it, saved their

faith, their marriages, and, sometimes literally, their lives.

In the first five chapters I will unlock the parable's basic meaning. In Chapter 6 I will demonstrate how the story helps us understand the Bible as a whole, and in Chapter 7 how its teaching works itself out in the way we live in the world.

I will not use the parable's most common name: the Parable of the Prodigal Son. It is not right to single out only one of the sons as the sole focus of the story. Even Jesus doesn't call it the Parable of *the* Prodigal Son, but begins the story saying, "a man had *two* sons." The narrative is as much about the elder brother as the younger, and as much about the father as the sons. And what Jesus says about the older brother is one of the most important messages given to us in the Bible. The parable might be better called the Two Lost Sons.

The word "prodigal" does not mean "wayward" but, according to *Merriam-Webster's Collegiate Dictionary,* "recklessly spendthrift." It means to spend

until you have nothing left. This term is therefore as appropriate for describing the father in the story as his younger son. The father's welcome to the repentant son was literally reckless, because he refused to "reckon" or count his sin against him or demand repayment. This response offended the elder son and most likely the local community.

In this story the father represents the Heavenly Father Jesus knew so well. St. Paul writes: "God was in Christ reconciling the world to himself, not reckoning to them their trespasses" (2 Corinthians 5:19—American Standard Version). Jesus is showing us the God of Great Expenditure, who is nothing if not prodigal toward us, his children. God's reckless grace is our greatest hope, a life-changing experience, and the subject of this book.

THE PRODIGAL GOD

prod-i-gal / prɒdɪgəl—adjective

   1. recklessly extravagant

   2. having spent everything

THE
PARABLE

LUKE 15: 1–3, 11–32

(Based on the New International Version, with some verses
translated by the author.)

1 Now the tax collectors and "sinners" were all gathering around to hear him. 2 But the Pharisees and the teachers of the law muttered, "This man welcomes sinners and eats with them." 3 Then Jesus told them this parable. . . .

11 Jesus continued, "There was a man who had two sons. 12 The younger one said to his father, 'Father, give me my share of the estate.' So he divided his property between them.

13 "Not long after that, the younger son got together all he had, set off for a far country

and there squandered his wealth in wild living. 14 After he had spent everything, there was a severe famine in that whole country, and he began to be in need. 15 So he went and hired himself out to a citizen of that country, who sent him to his fields to feed pigs. 16 He longed to fill his stomach with the pods that the pigs were eating, but no one gave him anything. 17 When he came to his senses, he said, 'How many of my father's hired men have food to spare, and here I am starving to death! 18 I will set out and go back to my father and say to him: Father, I have sinned against heaven and against you. 19 I am no longer worthy to be called your son; make me like one of your hired men.'

20 "So he got up and went to his father. But while he was still a long way off, his father saw him and was filled with compassion for him; he ran to his son, threw his arms around him

and kissed him. 21 The son said to him, 'Father, I have sinned against heaven and against you. I am no longer worthy to be called your son.'

22 "But the father said to his servants, 'Quick! Bring the best robe and put it on him. Put a ring on his finger and sandals on his feet. 23 Bring the fattened calf and kill it. Let's have a feast and celebrate. 24 For this son of mine was dead and is alive again; he was lost and is found.' So they began to celebrate.

25 "Meanwhile, the older son was in the field. When he came near the house, he heard music and dancing. 26 So he called one of the servants and asked him what was going on.

27 " 'Your brother has come,' he replied, 'and your father has killed the fattened calf because he has him back safe and sound.'

28 "The elder brother became angry and refused to go in. So his father went out and pleaded with him. 29 But he answered his father, 'Look! All these years I've been slaving for you and never disobeyed your orders. Yet you never gave me even a young goat so I could celebrate with my friends. 30 But when this son of yours who has squandered your property with prostitutes comes home, you kill the fattened calf for him!'

31 " 'My son,' the father said, 'you are always with me, and everything I have is yours. 32 But we had to celebrate and be glad, because this brother of yours was dead and is alive again; he was lost and is found.' "

ONE

✵✦✵✦✵

THE PEOPLE AROUND JESUS

"All gathering around to hear him."

Two Kinds of People

MOST readings of this parable have concentrated on the flight and return of the younger brother—the "Prodigal Son." That misses the real message of the story, however, because there are two brothers, each of whom represents a different way to be alienated from God, and a different way to seek acceptance into the kingdom of heaven.

It is crucial to notice the historical setting that the author provides for Jesus's teaching. In the first two verses of the chapter, Luke recounts that there were two groups of people who had come to listen to Jesus. First there were the "tax collectors and sin-

ners." These men and women correspond to the younger brother. They observed neither the moral laws of the Bible nor the rules for ceremonial purity followed by religious Jews. They engaged in "wild living." Like the younger brother, they "left home" by leaving the traditional morality of their families and of respectable society. The second group of listeners was the "Pharisees and the teachers of the law," who were represented by the elder brother. They held to the traditional morality of their upbringing. They studied and obeyed the Scripture. They worshipped faithfully and prayed constantly.

With great economy Luke shows how different each group's response was to Jesus. The progressive tense of the Greek verb translated "were gathering" conveys that the attraction of younger brothers to Jesus was an ongoing pattern in his ministry. They continually flocked to him. This phenomenon puzzled and angered the moral and the religious. Luke summarizes their complaint: "This man welcomes sinners and [even] eats with them." To sit down and eat with

someone in the ancient Near East was a token of acceptance. "How dare Jesus reach out to sinners like
that?" they were saying. "These people *never* come
to *our* services! Why would they be drawn to Jesus's
teaching? He couldn't be declaring the truth to them,
as we do. He *must* be just telling them what they want
to hear!"

So to whom is Jesus's teaching in this parable
directed? It is to the second group, the scribes and
Pharisees. It is in response to their attitude that Jesus
begins to tell the parable. The parable of the two
sons takes an extended look at the soul of the elder
brother, and climaxes with a powerful plea for him to
change his heart.

Throughout the centuries, when this text is taught
in church or religious education programs, the almost
exclusive focus has been on how the father freely re-
ceives his penitent younger son. The first time I heard
the parable, I imagined Jesus's original listeners' eyes
welling with tears as they heard how God will always
love and welcome them, no matter what they've done.

We sentimentalize this parable if we do that. The targets of this story are not "wayward sinners" but religious people who do everything the Bible requires. Jesus is pleading not so much with immoral outsiders as with moral insiders. He wants to show them their blindness, narrowness, and self-righteousness, and how these things are destroying both their own souls and the lives of the people around them. It is a mistake, then, to think that Jesus tells this story primarily to assure younger brothers of his unconditional love.

No, the original listeners were not melted into tears by this story but rather they were thunderstruck, offended, and infuriated. Jesus's purpose is not to warm our hearts but to shatter our categories. Through this parable Jesus challenges what nearly everyone has ever thought about God, sin, and salvation. His story reveals the destructive self-centeredness of the younger brother, but it also condemns the elder brother's moralistic life in the strongest terms. Jesus is saying that both the irreligious and the religious are

spiritually lost, both life-paths are dead ends, and that every thought the human race has had about how to connect to God has been wrong.

Why People Like Jesus but Not the Church

Both older brothers and younger brothers are with us today, in the same society and often in the very same family.

Frequently the oldest sibling in a family is the parent-pleaser, the responsible one who obeys the parental standards. The younger sibling tends to be the rebel, a free spirit who prefers the company and admiration of peers. The first child grows up, takes a conventional job, and settles down near Mom and Dad, while the younger sibling goes off to live in the hip-shabby neighborhoods of New York and Los Angeles.

These natural, temperamental differences have been accentuated in more recent times. In the early nineteenth century industrialization gave rise to a

new middle class—the bourgeois—which sought legitimacy through an ethic of hard work and moral rectitude. In response to perceived bourgeois hypocrisy and rigidity, communities of bohemians arose, from Henri Murger's 1840s Paris to the Bloomsbury Group of London, the Beats of Greenwich Village, and the indie-rock scenes of today. Bohemians stress freedom from convention and personal autonomy.

To some degree the so-called culture wars are playing out these same conflicting temperaments and impulses in modern society. More and more people today consider themselves non-religious or even anti-religious. They believe moral issues are highly complex and are suspicious of any individuals or institutions that claim moral authority over the lives of others. Despite (or perhaps because of) the rise of this secular spirit there has also been considerable growth in conservative, orthodox religious movements. Alarmed by what they perceive as an onslaught of moral relativism, many have organized to "take back the culture,"

and take as dim a view of "younger brothers" as the Pharisees did.

So whose side is Jesus on? In *The Lord of the Rings,* when the hobbits ask the ancient Treebeard whose side he is on, he answers: "I am not altogether on anybody's side, because nobody is altogether on my side. . . . [But] there are some things, of course, whose side I'm altogether *not* on."[3] Jesus's own answer to this question, through the parable, is similar. He is on the side of neither the irreligious nor the religious, but he singles out religious moralism as a particularly deadly spiritual condition.

It is hard for us to realize this today, but when Christianity first arose in the world it was not called a religion. It was the non-religion. Imagine the neighbors of early Christians asking them about their faith. "Where's your temple?" they'd ask. The Christians would reply that they didn't have a temple. "But how could that be? Where do your priests labor?" The Christians would have replied that they didn't have priests. "But . . . but," the neighbors would have

sputtered, "where are the sacrifices made to please your gods?" The Christians would have responded that they did not make sacrifices anymore. Jesus himself was the temple to end all temples, the priest to end all priests, and the sacrifice to end all sacrifices.[4]

No one had ever heard anything like this. So the Romans called them "atheists," because what the Christians were saying about spiritual reality was unique and could not be classified with the other religions of the world. This parable explains why they were absolutely right to call them atheists.

The irony of this should not be lost on us, standing as we do in the midst of the modern culture wars. To most people in our society, Christianity *is* religion and moralism. The only alternative to it (besides some other world religion) is pluralistic secularism. But from the beginning it was not so. Christianity was recognized as a *tertium quid*, something else entirely.

The crucial point here is that, in general, religiously observant people were offended by Jesus, but those estranged from religious and moral observance were

intrigued and attracted to him. We see this through-
out the New Testament accounts of Jesus's life. In
every case where Jesus meets a religious person and a
sexual outcast (as in Luke 7) or a religious person and
a racial outcast (as in John 3–4) or a religious person
and a political outcast (as in Luke 19), the outcast is
the one who connects with Jesus and the elder-brother
type does not. Jesus says to the respectable religious
leaders "the tax collectors and the prostitutes enter
the kingdom before you" (Matthew 21:31).

Jesus's teaching consistently attracted the irreligious while offending the Bible-believing, religious
people of his day. However, in the main, our churches
today do not have this effect. The kind of outsiders Jesus attracted are not attracted to contempo-
rary churches, even our most avant-garde ones. We
tend to draw conservative, buttoned-down, moralistic people. The licentious and liberated or the broken and marginal avoid church. That can only mean
one thing. If the preaching of our ministers and the
practice of our parishioners do not have the same

effect on people that Jesus had, then we must not be declaring the same message that Jesus did. If our churches aren't appealing to younger brothers, they must be more full of elder brothers than we'd like to think.

T W O

The Two Lost Sons

"There was a man who had two sons."

The Lost Younger Brother

J ESUS'S story might best be named the Parable of the Two Lost Sons. It is a drama in two acts, with Act 1 entitled "The Lost Younger Brother" and Act 2 "The Lost Elder Brother."

Act 1 begins with a short but shocking request. The younger son comes to the father and says, "Give me my share of the estate." The original listeners would have been amazed by such a request. Not that there was anything amiss in the son's expectation of a share of the family wealth. In those days when a father died the oldest son received a double portion of what the other children inherited. If a father had two heirs,

the oldest would have gotten two-thirds of the estate and the younger would have received one-third.

However, this division of the estate only occurred when the father died. Here the younger son asks for his inheritance *now,* which was a sign of deep disrespect. To ask this while the father still lived was the same as to wish him dead. The younger son was saying, essentially, that he wants his father's things, but not his father. His relationship to the father has been a means to the end of enjoying his wealth, and now he is weary of that relationship. He wants out. Now. "Give me what is mine," he says.

The father's response is even more startling than the request. This was an intensely patriarchal society, in which lavish expressions of deference and respect for elders and particularly for one's parents were of supreme importance. A traditional Middle Eastern father would be expected to respond to such a request by driving the son out of the family with nothing except physical blows. This father doesn't do anything like that. He simply "divided his property be-

tween them." To understand the significance of this, we should notice that the Greek word translated as "property" here is the word *bios,* which means "life." A more concrete word to denote capital could have been used but was not. Why not?

The wealth of this father would have primarily been in real estate, and to get one-third of his net worth he would have had to sell a great deal of his land holdings. In our mobile, urbanized culture we don't understand the relationship of the people in former generations to their land. Consider the line in the Rodgers and Hammerstein musical *Oklahoma!* "Oh, we know we belong to the land, and the land we belong to is grand!" Notice that it doesn't say the land belongs to them, but rather that they belong to *it*. This neatly sums up how in the past people's very identities were tied up in their place, their land. To lose part of your land was to lose part of yourself and a major share of your standing in the community. We have all heard stories of powerful and successful CEOs, both men and women, chucking their whole careers

in order to care for a hurting, needy child. While not an exact parallel, this is what the father does.

This younger brother, then, is asking his father to tear his life apart. And the father does so, for the love of his son. Most of Jesus's listeners would have never seen a Middle Eastern patriarch respond like this. The father patiently endures a tremendous loss of honor as well as the pain of rejected love. Ordinarily when our love is rejected we get angry, retaliate, and do what we can to diminish our affection for the rejecting person, so we won't hurt so much. But this father maintains his affection for his son and bears the agony.

The Younger Brother's Plan

Now we come to Scene 2 of Act 1. The son goes off to "a far country" and squanders everything he has through an out-of-control lifestyle. When he is literally down in the mud with the pigs, he "comes to his senses" and devises a plan. First, he says to himself, he will return to his father and admit that he was wrong

The Two Lost Sons

and that he has forfeited the right to be his son. But secondly he intends to ask his father to "make me like one of your hired men."

This is a very specific request. Servants worked on the estate and lived there. But "hired men" were various kinds of tradesmen and craftsmen who lived in local villages and earned a wage. Many commentators believe that the son's strategy went something like this. The younger son had disgraced his family and therefore the whole community. He was "dead" to them, as the father describes it. The rabbis taught that if you had violated the community's standards an apology was not sufficient—you also had to make restitution. The son intends to say: "Father, I know I don't have a right to come back into the family. But if you apprentice me to one of your hired men so I can learn a trade and earn a wage, then at least I could begin to pay off my debt." That was his plan. There in the pigsty the younger son rehearses his speech. When he feels he is ready for the confrontation, he picks up and begins the journey home.

THE PRODIGAL GOD

We come to the dramatic third and final scene of Act 1. The younger son comes within sight of the house. His father sees him and runs—*runs* to him! As a general rule, distinguished Middle Eastern patriarchs did not run. Children might run; women might run; young men might run. But not the paterfamilias, the dignified pillar of the community, the owner of the great estate. He would not pick up his robes and bare his legs like some boy. But this father does. He runs to his son and, showing his emotions openly, falls upon him and kisses him.

This almost surely would have taken the younger brother by surprise. Flummoxed, he tries to roll out his business plan for the restitution. The father interrupts him, not only ignoring his rehearsed speech, but directly contradicting it. "Quick!" he says to his servants. "Bring the best robe and put it on him!" What is he saying?

The best robe in the house would have been the father's own robe, the unmistakable sign of restored standing in the family. The father is saying, "I'm not

going to wait until you've paid off your debt; I'm not going to wait until you've duly groveled. <u>You are not going to earn your way back into the family, I am going to simply take you back</u>. I will cover your nakedness, poverty, and rags with the robes of my office and honor."

He commands that the servants prepare a feast of celebration, with "the fattened calf" as the main course. In that society, most meals did not include meat, which was an expensive delicacy. Meat was often reserved for special occasions and parties. But no meat was more expensive than the fattened calf. To throw such a feast would have been something that happened only on the rarest of occasions, and likely the entire village was invited. Word spread quickly, and soon there was a full-fledged feast going on, with music and dancing, all to celebrate the restoration of the younger son to life, family, and community.

What a scene! The father has yet to deal with the much more complicated and poisonous spiritual condition of the elder brother in Act 2. But Act 1 already

challenges the mind-set of elder brothers with a star-tling message: God's love and forgiveness can pardon and restore any and every kind of sin or wrongdoing. It doesn't matter who you are or what you've done. It doesn't matter if you've deliberately oppressed or even murdered people, or how much you've abused yourself. The younger brother knew that in his father's house there was abundant "food to spare," but he also discovered that there was grace to spare. There is no evil that the father's love cannot pardon and cover, there is no sin that is a match for his grace.

Act 1, then, demonstrates the lavish prodigality of God's grace. Jesus shows the father pouncing on his son in love not only before he has a chance to clean up his life and evidence a change of heart, but even before he can recite his repentance speech. Nothing, not even abject contrition, merits the favor of God. The Father's love and acceptance are absolutely free.

For all its beauty, however, Act 1 cannot stand alone. There are many commentators who, focus-ing exclusively on Act 1, conclude that this parable

contradicts traditional Christian doctrine. "Look," they say, "there is no mention of atonement for sin. There's no need for a savior on a cross that pays for sin. God is a God of universal love who unconditionally accepts everyone, no matter what."

If that were the message, Jesus would have ended the narrative there. But he did not, because it is not. While Act 1 shows us the freeness of God's grace, Act 2 will show us the costliness of that grace and the true climax of the story.

The Lost Elder Brother

When the elder brother hears from the servants that his younger brother has returned and has been reinstated by his father, he is furious. Now it is his turn to disgrace the father.

He refuses to go in to what is perhaps the biggest feast and public event his father has ever put on. He remains outside the door, publicly casting a vote of no-confidence in his father's actions. This forces the

father to come out to speak to his older son, a demeaning thing to have to do when you are the lord of the manor and host of a great feast. He begins to plead with his eldest son to come in, but he continues to refuse.

Why is the older son so furious? He is especially upset about the cost of all that is happening. He says, "You've never given me even a goat for a party, how dare you give him the calf?" The fattened calf is only a symbol, however, because what the father has done costs far more than the calf. By bringing the younger brother back into the family he has made him an heir again, with a claim to one-third of their (now very diminished) family wealth. This is unconscionable to the elder brother. He's adding things up. "I've worked myself to death and earned what I've got, but my brother has done *nothing* to earn anything, indeed he's merited only expulsion, and yet you lavish him with wealth! Where's the justice in that?" That is why the elder brother refers to his record. "I have never disobeyed you! So I have rights!" he is saying. "I de-

The Two Lost Sons

serve to be consulted about this! You have no right to make these decisions unilaterally."

And so the elder brother's fury leads him to insult the father even further. He refuses to address him in the elaborately respectful manner that inferiors owed superiors in that culture, particularly in public. He does not say "esteemed father" but simply, "Look!"—which is equivalent to "Look, you!" In a culture where respect and deference to elders was all important, such behavior is outrageous. A modern-day equivalent might be a son writing a humiliating tell-all memoir that destroys his father's reputation and career.

Finally we come to the denouement. How will the father respond to his older son's open rebellion? What will he do? A man of his time and place might have disowned his son on the spot. Instead he responds again with amazing tenderness. "My son," he begins, "despite how you've insulted me publicly, I still want you in the feast. I am not going to disown your brother, but I don't want to disown you, either. I challenge

you to swallow your pride and come into the feast. The choice is yours. Will you, or will you not?" It is an unexpectedly gracious, dramatic appeal.

The listeners are on the edge of their seats. Will the family finally be reunited in unity and love? Will the brothers be reconciled? Will the elder brother be softened by this remarkable offer and be reconciled to the father?

Just as all these thoughts pass through our mind, the story ends! Why doesn't Jesus finish the story and tell us what happened?! It is because the real audience for this story is the Pharisees, the elder brothers. Jesus is pleading with his enemies to respond to his message. What is that message? The answer to that question will emerge as we take time in the next chapters to understand the main points Jesus is seeking to drive home here. In short, Jesus is redefining everything we thought we knew about connecting to God. He is redefining sin, what it means to be lost, and what it means to be saved.

THREE

REDEFINING SIN

"All these years I've been slaving for you."

Two Ways to Find Happiness

JESUS uses the younger and elder brothers to portray the two basic ways people try to find happiness and fulfillment: the way of *moral conformity* and the way of *self-discovery*. Each acts as a lens coloring how you see all of life, or as a paradigm shaping your understanding of everything. Each is a way of finding personal significance and worth, of addressing the ills of the world, and of determining right from wrong.

The elder brother in the parable illustrates the way of moral conformity. The Pharisees of Jesus's day believed that, while they were a people chosen by God, they could only maintain their place in his blessing

and receive final salvation through strict obedience to the Bible. There are innumerable varieties of this paradigm, but they all believe in putting the will of God and the standards of the community ahead of individual fulfillment. In this view, we only attain happiness and a world made right by achieving moral rectitude. We may fall at times, of course, but then we will be judged by how abject and intense our regret is. In this view, even in our failures we must always measure up.

The younger brother in the parable illustrates the way of self-discovery. In ancient patriarchal cultures some took this route, but there are far more who do so today. This paradigm holds that individuals must be free to pursue their own goals and self-actualization regardless of custom and convention. In this view, the world would be a far better place if tradition, prejudice, hierarchical authority, and other barriers to personal freedom were weakened or removed.

These two ways of life (and their inevitable clash) are vividly depicted in the classic movie *Witness*. In that story, the young Amish widow Rachel falls in love

with the decidedly non-Amish policeman, John Book. Her father-in-law, Eli, warns her that it is forbidden to do so and that the elders could have her punished. He adds that she is acting like a child. "I will be the judge of that," she retorts. "No, *they* will be the judge of that. And so will I . . . if you shame me," he says, fierce as a prophet. "You shame yourself," Rachel replies, shaken but proud, and turns away from him.[5]

Here we have a concise portrayal of the two ways. The person in the way of moral conformity says: "I'm not going to do what I want, but what tradition and the community wants me to do." The person choosing the way of self-discovery says: "I'm the only one who can decide what is right or wrong for me. I'm going to live as I want to live and find my true self and happiness that way."

Our Western society is so deeply divided between these two approaches that hardly anyone can conceive of any other way to live. If you criticize or distance yourself from one, everyone assumes you have chosen to follow the other, because each of these approaches

tends to divide the whole world into two basic groups. The moral conformists say: "The immoral people—the people who 'do their own thing'—are the problem with the world, and moral people are the solution." The advocates of self-discovery say: "The bigoted people—the people who say, 'We have the Truth'—are the problem with the world, and progressive people are the solution." Each side says: "Our way is the way the world will be put to rights, and if you are not with us, you are against us."

Are we to conclude that everyone falls into one or the other of these two categories? Yes and no. A great number of people have temperaments that predispose them to either a life of moral conformity or of self-discovery. Some, however, go back and forth, trying first one strategy and then the other in different seasons of their lives. Many have tried the moral conformity paradigm, found it crushed them, and in a dramatic turn moved into a life of self-discovery. Others are on the opposite trajectory.

Some people combine both approaches under the

roof of the same personality. There are some traditional-looking elder brothers that, as a release valve, maintain a secret life of younger-brother behavior. Police sting operations, designed to catch Internet sexual predators who seek out young teens, regularly catch highly religious people in their nets, including many clergy. Then again, there are many people, very liberated and irreligious in their views and lifestyle, who regard religious conservatives with all the self-righteousness and condescension of the worst Pharisee.

Despite these variations, these are still only two primary approaches to living. The message of Jesus's parable is that both of these approaches are wrong. His parable illustrates the radical alternative.

Two Lost Sons

In Act 1, in the person of the younger brother, Jesus gives us a depiction of sin that anyone would recognize. The young man humiliates his family and lives a self-indulgent, dissolute life. He is totally out of con-

trol. He is alienated from the father, who represents God in the story. Anyone who lives like that would be cut off from God, as all the listeners to the parable would have agreed.

In Act 2, however, the focus is on the elder brother. He is fastidiously obedient to his father and, therefore, by analogy, to the commands of God. He is completely under control and quite self-disciplined. So we have two sons, one "bad" by conventional standards and one "good," yet both are alienated from the father. The father has to go out and invite each of them to come into the feast of his love. <u>So there is not just one lost son in this parable—there are two</u>.

But Act 2 comes to an unthinkable conclusion. Jesus the storyteller deliberately leaves the elder brother in his alienated state. The bad son enters the father's feast but the good son will not. The lover of prostitutes is saved, but the man of moral rectitude is still lost. We can almost hear the Pharisees gasp as the story ends. It was the complete reversal of everything they had ever been taught.

Redefining Sin

Jesus does not simply leave it at that. It gets even more shocking. Why doesn't the elder brother go in? He himself gives the reason: "Because I've never disobeyed you." The elder brother is not losing the father's love in spite of his goodness, but *because* of it. It is not his sins that create the barrier between him and his father, it's the pride he has in his moral record; it's not his wrongdoing but his righteousness that is keeping him from sharing in the feast of the father.

How could this be? The answer is that the brothers' hearts, and the two ways of life they represent, are much more alike than they first appear.

What did the younger son most want in life? He chafed at having to partake of his family's assets under the father's supervision. He wanted to make his own decisions and have unfettered control of his portion of the wealth. How did he get that? He did it with a bold power play, a flagrant defiance of community standards, a declaration of complete independence.

What did the older son most want? If we think about it we realize that he wanted the same thing as

his brother. He was just as resentful of the father as was the younger son. He, too, wanted the father's goods rather than the father himself. However, while the younger brother went far away, the elder brother stayed close and "never disobeyed." That was his way to get control. His unspoken demand is, "I have never disobeyed you! Now you have to do things in my life the way I want them to be done."

The hearts of the two brothers were the same. Both sons resented their father's authority and sought ways of getting out from under it. They each wanted to get into a position in which they could tell the father what to do. Each one, in other words, rebelled—but one did so by being very bad and the other by being extremely good. Both were alienated from the father's heart; both were lost sons.

Do you realize, then, what Jesus is teaching? Neither son loved the father for himself. They both were using the father for their own self-centered ends rather than loving, enjoying, and serving him for his own sake. This means that you can rebel against God

and be <u>alienated from him either by breaking his rules</u> <u>or by keeping all of them diligently</u>.

It's a shocking message: Careful obedience to God's law may serve as a strategy for rebelling against God.

A Deeper Understanding of Sin

With this parable Jesus gives us a much deeper concept of "sin" than any of us would have if he didn't supply it. Most people think of sin as failing to keep God's rules of conduct, but, while not less than that, Jesus's definition of sin goes beyond it.

In her novel *Wise Blood*, Flannery O'Connor says of her character Hazel Motes that "<u>there was a deep,</u> <u>black, wordless conviction in him that the way to</u> <u>avoid Jesus was to avoid sin.</u>"[6] <u>This is a profound insight. You can avoid Jesus as Savior by keeping all the moral laws</u>. If you do that, then you have "rights." God owes you answered prayers, and a good life, and a ticket to heaven when you die. You don't need a

Savior who pardons you by free grace, for you are your own Savior.

This attitude is clearly that of the elder brother. Why is he so angry with the father? He feels he has the right to tell the father how the robes, rings, and livestock of the family should be deployed. In the same way, religious people commonly live very moral lives, but their goal is to get leverage over God, to control him, to put him in a position where they think he owes them. Therefore, despite all their ethical fastidiousness and piety, they are actually rebelling against his authority. If, like the elder brother, you believe that God ought to bless you and help you because you have worked so hard to obey him and be a good person, then Jesus may be your helper, your example, even your inspiration, but he is not your Savior. You are serving as your own Savior.

Underneath the brothers' sharply different patterns of behavior is the same motivation and aim. Both are using the father in different ways to get the things on which their hearts are really fixed. It was the

wealth, not the love of the father, that they believed would make them happy and fulfilled.

At the end of the story, the elder brother has an opportunity to truly delight the father by going into the feast. But his resentful refusal shows that the father's happiness had never been his goal. When the father reinstates the younger son, to the diminishment of the older son's share in the estate, the elder brother's heart is laid bare. He does everything he can to hurt and resist his father.

If, like the elder brother, you seek to control God through your obedience, then all your morality is just a way to use God to make him give you the things in life you really want. A classic example of this is the bargain that the young Salieri makes with God in Peter Shaffer's play *Amadeus*.

I would offer up secretly the proudest prayer a boy could think of. "Lord, make me a great composer! Let me celebrate your glory through music—and be celebrated myself! Make me fa-

mous through the world, dear God! Make me immortal! After I die let people speak my name forever with love for what I wrote! In return I vow I will give you my chastity, my industry, my deepest humility, every hour of my life. And I will help my fellow man all I can. Amen and amen!"

He begins a life under this vow to God. He keeps his hands off women, works diligently at his music, teaches many musicians for free, and tirelessly helps the poor. His career goes well and he believes God is keeping his end of the bargain. Then Mozart appears with musical gifts far above Salieri's. His genius had obviously been bestowed on him by God. Amadeus, Mozart's middle name, means "beloved by God," and yet he is a vulgar, self-indulgent "younger brother." The talent God lavished so prodigally on Mozart precipitates a crisis of faith in the elder-brother heart of Salieri. His words are remarkably close to those of the older son in the parable:

Redefining Sin

It was incomprehensible. . . . Here I was denying all my natural lust in order to deserve God's gift and there was Mozart indulging his in all directions—even though engaged to be married—and no rebuke at all!

Finally, Salieri says to God, "From now on we are enemies, You and I," and thereafter works to destroy Mozart.[7] Sadly, in Shaffer's play, God is silent, unlike the father in Jesus's parable, who reaches out to rescue the elder brother even as he begins to sink into the bitterness, hate, and despair that eventually swallows Salieri.

Salieri's diligent efforts to be chaste and charitable were ultimately revealed to be profoundly self-interested. God and the poor were just useful instruments. He told himself that he was sacrificing his time and money for the poor's sake and for God's sake, but there was actually no sacrifice involved. He was doing it for his own sake, to get fame, fortune, and self-esteem. "I liked myself," Salieri said, ". . . Till

he came. Mozart." The minute he realized that his service to God and the poor wasn't gaining him the glory he craved so deeply, his heart became murderous. Soon the moral and respectable Salieri shows himself capable of greater evil than the immoral, vulgar Mozart. While the Mozart of *Amadeus* is irreligious, it is Salieri the devout who ends up in a much greater state of alienation from God, just like in Jesus's parable.

This mind-set can be present in more subtle form than it was in the life of Salieri. I knew a woman who had worked for many years in Christian ministry. When chronic illness overtook her in middle age, it threw her into despair. Eventually she realized that deep in her heart she had felt that God owed her a better life, after all she had done for him. That assumption made it extremely difficult for her to climb out of her pit, though climb she did. The key to her improvement, however, was to recognize the elder-brother mind-set within.

Elder brothers obey God to get things. They don't

obey God to get God himself—in order to resemble him, love him, know him, and delight him. So religious and moral people can be avoiding Jesus as Savior and Lord as much as the younger brothers who say they don't believe in God and define right and wrong for themselves.

Here, then, is Jesus's radical redefinition of what is wrong with us. Nearly everyone defines sin as breaking a list of rules. Jesus, though, shows us that a man who has violated virtually nothing on the list of moral misbehaviors can be every bit as spiritually lost as the most profligate, immoral person. Why? Because sin is not just breaking the rules, it is putting yourself in the place of God as Savior, Lord, and Judge just as each son sought to displace the authority of the father in his own life.

The young Salieri would have objected strongly if someone had told him he was doing this. By being chaste and charitable was he not doing God's will rather than his own, was he not honoring and submitting to God? But by seeking to put God in his debt

and get control over him through his good works—instead of relying on his sheer grace—he was acting as his own Savior. When he became murderously bitter toward Mozart, certain that God was being unjust, he was putting himself in the place of God the Judge.

There are two ways to be your own Savior and Lord. One is by breaking all the moral laws and setting your own course, and one is by keeping all the moral laws and being very, very good.

Both Wrong; Both Loved

Jesus does not divide the world into the moral "good guys" and the immoral "bad guys." He shows us that everyone is dedicated to a project of self-salvation, to using God and others in order to get power and control for themselves. We are just going about it in different ways. Even though both sons are wrong, however, the father cares for them and invites them both back into his love and feast.

This means that Jesus's message, which is "the gos-

pel," is a completely different spirituality. The gospel of Jesus is not religion or irreligion, morality or immorality, moralism or relativism, conservatism or liberalism. Nor is it something halfway along a spectrum between two poles—it is something else altogether.

The gospel is distinct from the other two approaches: In its view, everyone is wrong, everyone is loved, and everyone is called to recognize this and change. By contrast, elder brothers divide the world in two: "The good people (like us) are in and the bad people, who are the real problem with the world, are out." Younger brothers, even if they don't believe in God at all, do the same thing, saying: "No, the open-minded and tolerant people are in and the bigoted, narrow-minded people, who are the real problem with the world, are out."

But Jesus says: "The humble are in and the proud are out" (see Luke 18:14).[8] The people who confess they aren't particularly good or open-minded are moving toward God, because the prerequisite for receiving the grace of God is to know you need it. The

people who think they are just fine, thank you, are moving away from God. "The Lord . . . cares for the humble, but he keeps his distance from the proud" (Psalm 138:6—New Living Translation).

When a newspaper posed the question, "What's Wrong with the World?" the Catholic thinker G. K. Chesterton reputedly wrote a brief letter in response: "Dear Sirs: I am. Sincerely Yours, G. K. Chesterton." That is the attitude of someone who has grasped the message of Jesus.

Although the sons are both wrong and both loved, the story does not end on the same note for each. Why does Jesus construct the story so that one of them is saved, restored to a right relationship with the father, and one of them is not? (At least, not before the story ends.) It may be that Jesus is trying to say that while both forms of the self-salvation project are equally wrong, each one is not equally dangerous. One of the ironies of the parable is now revealed. The younger son's flight from the father was crashingly obvious. He left the father literally, physically, and

morally. Though the older son stayed at home, he was actually more distant and alienated from the father than his brother, because he was blind to his true condition. He would have been horribly offended by the suggestion that he was rebelling against the father's authority and love, but he was, deeply.

Because the elder brother is more blind to what is going on, being an elder-brother Pharisee is a more spiritually desperate condition. "How dare you say that?" is how religious people respond if you suggest their relationship with God isn't right. "I'm there every time the church doors are open." Jesus says, in effect, "That doesn't matter."

No one had ever taught anything like this before.

FOUR

❖❖❖

REDEFINING LOSTNESS

"The older brother became angry and refused to go in."

Anger and Superiority

JESUS often speaks of sin and salvation under the metaphors of being "lost" and "found." Chapter 15 of Luke's gospel contains three parables that Jesus tells to the religious leaders. The first is about a shepherd who discovers that one of his sheep is lost. The second parable is about a woman who discovers that one of her coins is lost. As we have seen, the third parable is about two sons who are, in different ways, both lost. Elsewhere, Jesus summarizes his ministry as a rescue operation, coming "to seek and save that which is lost" (Luke 19:10).

What does it mean to be spiritually lost? In the

[48]

parable, the younger brother's lostness is clearly seen when he ends up in the pigsty. He has run out of friends, money, and resources because of his self-indulgent, undisciplined, and foolish behavior. It has led to a complete life collapse. At that point, the younger brother realizes that he has "lost his way" and returns to try to rebuild his life.

However, in this parable Jesus wants us to discern another, more subtle, but no less devastating form of lostness. Once we have Jesus's deeper definition of sin we should be able to recognize it, and it is crucial that we do. We will call it "elder-brother lostness." It brings as much misery and strife into the world as the other kind. A closer look at the elder brother helps us discern its features.

We see that the elder brother "became angry." All of his words are dripping with resentment. <u>The first sign you have an elder-brother spirit is that when your life doesn't go as you want, you aren't just sorrowful but deeply angry and bitter</u>. Elder brothers believe that if they live a good life they should get a good life,

that God owes them a smooth road if they try very hard to live up to standards.

What happens, then, if you are an elder brother and things go wrong in your life? If you feel you have been living up to your moral standards, you will be furious with God. You don't deserve this, you will think, after how hard you've worked to be a decent person! What happens, however, if things have gone wrong in your life when you know that you have been falling short of your standards? Then you will be furious with yourself, filled with self-loathing and inner pain. And if evil circumstances overtake you, and you are not sure whether your life has been good enough or not, you may swing miserably back and forth between the poles of "I hate Thee!" and "I hate me."

Elder brothers' inability to handle suffering arises from the fact that their moral observance is results-oriented. The good life is lived not for delight in good deeds themselves, but as calculated ways to control their environment.

Elisabeth Elliot recounts an apocryphal story (not

in the Bible!) about Jesus that conveys the difference between a results-oriented selfishness and a faithful-ness born of love.

One day Jesus said to his disciples: "I'd like you to carry a stone for Me." He didn't give any explanation. So the disciples looked around for a stone to carry, and Peter, being the practical sort, sought out the smallest stone he could possibly find. After all, Jesus didn't give any regulations for weight and size! So he put it in his pocket. Jesus then said: "Follow Me." He led them on a journey. About noontime Jesus had everyone sit down. He waved his hands and all the stones turned to bread. He said, "Now it's time for lunch." In a few seconds, Peter's lunch was over. When lunch was done Jesus told them to stand up. He said again, "I'd like you to carry a stone for Me." This time Peter said, "Aha! Now I get it!" So he looked around and saw a small boulder. He hoisted it on his back

and it was painful, it made him stagger. But he said, "I can't wait for supper." Jesus then said: "Follow Me." He led them on a journey, with Peter barely being able to keep up. Around supper time Jesus led them to the side of a river. He said, "Now everyone throw your stones into the water." They did. Then he said, "Follow Me," and began to walk. Peter and the others looked at him dumbfounded. Jesus sighed and said, "Don't you remember what I asked you to do? Who were you carrying the stone *for*?"[9]

Like Peter, elder brothers expect their goodness to pay off, and if it doesn't, there is confusion and rage. If you think goodness and decency is the way to merit a good life from God, you will be eaten up with anger, since life never goes as we wish. You will always feel that you are owed more than you are getting. You will always see someone doing better than you in some aspect of life and will ask, "Why this person and not me? After all I've done!" This resentment is your own

fault. It is caused not by the prosperity of the other person, but by your own effort to control life through your performance. The strong undertow of anger this causes may not turn you into a murderer, as it did Salieri, but it will constantly cause you to lose your footing in various ways.

We also see that <u>the elder brother has a strong sense of his own superiority</u>. He points out how much better his own moral record is than the lover of prostitutes. In disdainful language ("This son of yours . . .") he won't even own his brother as a brother anymore.

Elder brothers base their self-images on being hardworking, or moral, or members of an elite clan, or extremely smart and savvy. This inevitably leads to feeling superior to those who don't have those same qualities. In <u>fact, competitive comparison is the main way elder brothers achieve a sense of their own significance</u>. Racism and classism are just different versions of this form of the self-salvation project. This dynamic becomes exceptionally intense when elder

brothers pride themselves above all for their right religion. If a group believes God favors them because of their particularly true doctrine, ways of worship, and ethical behavior, their attitude toward those without these things can be hostile. Their self-righteousness hides under the claim that they are only opposing the enemies of God. When you look at the world through those lenses, it becomes easy to justify hate and oppression, all in the name of truth. As Richard Lovelace has written:

> "[People] who are no longer sure that God loves and accepts them in Jesus, apart from their present spiritual achievements, are subconsciously radically insecure persons. . . . Their insecurity shows itself in pride, a fierce, defensive assertion of their own righteousness, and defensive criticism of others. They come naturally to hate other cultural styles and other races in order to bolster their own security and discharge their suppressed anger."[10]

Redefining Lostness

Elder brother self-righteousness not only creates racism and classism, but at the personal level creates an unforgiving, ~~judgmental spirit~~. This elder brother cannot pardon his younger brother for the way he has weakened the family's place in society, disgraced their name, and diminished their wealth. He highlights the fact that the younger brother has been with "prostitutes," while he has been living a chaste life at home. "I would *never* do anything as bad as that!" he is saying in his heart. Because he does not see himself as being part of a common community of sinners, he is trapped by his own bitterness. <u>It is impossible to forgive someone if you feel superior to him or her</u>. *mark of true forgiveness – humility*

If you can't control your temper, and you see someone else losing theirs in exactly the same way that you do, you tend to forgive them, because you know you are no better a person than they. How can I hold this against them when I am just as bad? you think. However, because elder brothers' sin and antipathy to God is hidden deep beneath layers of self-control and

moral behavior, they have no trouble feeling superior to just about anyone. If they see people who lie, or cheat on their wives, or don't pray to God—they look down on them. If such people wrong *them*, elder brothers feel their spotless record gives them the right to be highly offended and to perpetually remind the wrongdoer of his or her failure.

A classic example of this is the marriage of an alcoholic. The alcoholic repeatedly lets down his family in dramatic ways. As a result of her suffering, the addict's wife often develops an enormous amount of self-pity and self-righteousness. The spouse bails him out and yet holds the record of his sins constantly over his head. This leads to more self-loathing on the part of the alcoholic, which is part of why he drinks. It is a seductive, destructive cycle. It may be that the elder brother, to bolster his own image of himself, needed a chronically wayward sibling to criticize, and the smug older brother only made it harder for the younger to admit his problems and change his life. When the younger son comes out of his denial,

and the father welcomes him, the elder brother realizes that the pattern is being broken, and his fury is white-hot.

If the elder brother had known his own heart, he would have said, "I am just as self-centered and a grief to my father in my own way as my brother is in his. I have no right to feel superior." Then he would have had the freedom to give his brother the same forgiveness that his father did. But elder brothers do not see themselves this way. Their anger is a prison of their own making.

Slavishness and Emptiness

Another sign of those with an "elder brother" spirit is joyless, fear-based compliance. The older son boasts of his obedience to his father, but lets his underlying motivation and attitude slip out when he says, "All these years I've been slaving for you." To be sure, being faithful to any commitment involves a certain amount of dutifulness. Often we don't feel like doing

what we ought to do, but we do it anyway, for the sake of integrity. But the elder brother shows that his obedience to his father is nothing but duty all the way down. There is no joy or love, no reward in just seeing his father pleased.

In the same way, elder brothers are fastidious in their compliance to ethical norms, and in fulfillment of all traditional family, community, and civic responsibilities. But it is a slavish, joyless drudgery. The word "slave" has strong overtones of being forced or pushed rather than drawn or attracted. A slave works out of fear—fear of consequences imposed by force. This gets to the root of what drives an elder brother. Ultimately, elder brothers live good lives out of fear, not out of joy and love.

A friend who attended a prestigious MBA program once told me about the business ethics course he took there. The professor counseled honest business practices for two reasons. First, if you lie or cheat you may be caught, and that would be bad for business. Second, if people in the company know they

are working in an honest business, that will boost morale, making your employees feel they are above the competition. Indeed, these are good reasons to be honest, but this appeal only arouses the motives of fear, that they might lose profits, and pride, that they would feel superior to others around them. "Tell the truth—because it's to your own advantage," was the counsel.

What happens, however, when you inevitably come to situations in which telling the truth would cost you dearly? What happens when telling a particular lie would be stupendously advantageous to you? At those points, your motivation for honesty will evaporate. Some of the biggest corporate scandals of the last decade have involved devout, prominent church members.

Elder-brother obedience only leads to a slavish, begrudging compliance to the letter of the law. It is one thing to be honest and avoid lies for your sake, but it is another to do so for God's sake, for truth's sake, and for the love of the people around us. A per-

son motivated by love rather than fear will not only obey the letter of the law, but will eagerly seek out new ways to carry out business with transparency and integrity.

Honesty born of fear does nothing to root out the fundamental cause of evil in the world—the radical self-centeredness of the human heart. If anything, fear-based morality strengthens it, since ultimately elder brothers are being moral only for their own benefit. They may be kind to others and helpful to the poor, but at a deeper level they are doing it either so God will bless them, in the religious version of elder brotherness, or so they can think of themselves as virtuous, charitable persons, in the secular version of it. Here is a story that illustrates this:

> Once upon a time there was a gardener who grew an enormous carrot. So he took it to his king and said, "My lord, this is the greatest carrot I've ever grown or ever will grow. Therefore I want to present it to you as a token of my love

and respect for you." The king was touched and discerned the man's heart, so as he turned to go the king said, "Wait! You are clearly a good steward of the earth. I own a plot of land right next to yours. I want to give it to you freely as a gift so you can garden it all." And the gardener was amazed and delighted and went home rejoicing. But there was a nobleman at the king's court who overheard all this. And he said, "My! If that is what you get for a *carrot*—what if you gave the king something better?" So the next day the nobleman came before the king and he was leading a handsome black stallion. He bowed low and said, "My lord, I breed horses and this is the greatest horse I've ever bred or ever will. Therefore I want to present it to you as a token of my love and respect for you." But the king discerned his heart and said thank you, and took the horse and merely dismissed him. The nobleman was perplexed. So the king said, "Let me explain. That gardener was giving *me*

the carrot, but you were giving your*self* the horse."

Elder brothers may do good to others, but not out of delight in the deeds themselves or for the love of people or the pleasure of God. They are not really feeding the hungry and clothing the poor, they are feeding and clothing themselves. The heart's fundamental self-centeredness is not only kept intact but nurtured by fear-based moralism. This can and does erupt in shocking ways. Why do you think so many churches are plagued with gossip and fighting? Or why do so many moral people live apparently chaste lives and then suddenly fall into the most scandalous sins? Underneath the seeming unselfishness is great self-centeredness.

Religious and moral duties are a great burden, often a crushing one. Emotional frustration and inner boredom with life is repressed and denied. Elder brothers are under great pressure to appear, even to themselves, happy and content. This is the reason that

sometimes highly moral elder brothers will blow up their lives and, to the shock of all who know them, throw off the chains of their obligations and begin living like younger brothers.

The last sign of the elder-brother spirit is a lack of assurance of the father's love. The older son says, "You never threw *me* a party." There is no dancing or festiveness about the elder brother's relationship with his father. As long as you are trying to earn your salvation by controlling God through goodness, you will never be sure you have been good enough for him. You simply aren't sure God loves and delights in you.

What are the signs of this lack of assurance? We have already mentioned one sign: Every time something goes wrong in your life or a prayer goes unanswered, you wonder if it's because you aren't living right in this or that area. Another sign is that criticism from others doesn't just hurt your feelings, it devastates you. This is because your sense of God's love is abstract and has little real power in your life, and you

need the approval of others to bolster your sense of value. You will also feel irresolvable guilt. When you do something you know is wrong, your conscience torments you for a long time, even after you repent. Since you can't be sure you've repented deeply enough, you beat yourself up over what you did.

But perhaps the clearest symptom of this lack of assurance is a dry prayer life. Though elder brothers may be diligent in prayer, there is no wonder, awe, intimacy, or delight in their conversations with God. Think of three kinds of people—a business associate you don't really like, a friend you enjoy doing things with, and someone you are in love with, and who is in love with you. Your conversations with the business associate will be quite goal-oriented. You won't be interested in chitchat. With your friend you may open your heart about some of the problems you are having. But with your lover you will sense a strong impulse to speak about what you find beautiful about him or her.

These three kinds of discourse are analogous to

forms of prayer that have been called "petition," "confession," and "adoration." The deeper the love relationship, the more the conversation heads toward the personal, and toward affirmation and praise. Elder brothers may be disciplined in observing regular times of prayer, but their prayers are almost wholly taken up with a recitation of needs and petitions, not spontaneous, joyful praise. In fact, many elder brothers, for all their religiosity, do not have much of a private prayer life at all unless things are not going well in their lives. Then they may devote themselves to a great deal of it, until things get better again. This reveals that their main goal in prayer is to control their environment rather than to delve into an intimate relationship with a God who loves them.

Who Needs to Know This?

Why is it so important to know that Jesus exposes elder-brother lostness as being as wrong and destructive as younger-brother lostness?

The elder brothers of the world desperately need to see themselves in this mirror. Jesus aimed this parable primarily at the Pharisees, to show them who they were and to urge them to change. As we said, the younger brother knew he was alienated from the father, but the elder brother did not. That's why elder-brother lostness is so dangerous. Elder brothers don't go to God and beg for healing from their condition. They see nothing wrong with their condition, and that can be fatal. If you know you are sick you may go to a doctor; if you don't know you're sick you won't—you'll just die.

The younger brothers of the world also desperately need to see this. When we see the attitude of the elder brother in the story we begin to realize one of the reasons the younger brother wanted to leave in the first place. There are many people today who have abandoned any kind of religious faith because they see clearly that the major religions are simply full of elder brothers. They have come to the conclusion that religion is one of the greatest sources of misery and strife

in the world. And guess what? Jesus says through this parable—they are right. ~~The anger and superiority of elder brothers, all growing out of insecurity, fear, and inner emptiness, can create a huge body of guilt-ridden, fear-ridden, spiritually blind people, which is one of the great sources of social injustice, war, and violence.~~

It is typical for people who have turned their backs on religion to believe that Christianity is no different. They have been in churches brimming with elder-brother types. They say, "Christianity is just another religion." But Jesus says, no, that is not true. Everybody knows that the Christian gospel calls us away from the licentiousness of younger brotherness, but few realize that it also condemns moralistic elder brotherness.

Our big cities are filled with younger brothers who fled from churches in the heartland that were dominated by elder brothers. When I moved to New York City in the late 1980s to begin a new church, I thought I would meet many secular people who

had no familiarity with Christianity at all. I did, but to my surprise I met just as many people who had been raised in churches and in devout families and had come to New York City to get as far away from them as possible. After about a year of ministry we had two or three hundred people attending services. I was asked, "Who is coming to your church?" Upon reflection, I answered that it was about one-third non-believers, one-third believers, and one-third "recovering" believers—younger brothers. I ~~had met so many younger brothers who had been hurt and offended by elder brothers that neither they nor I were sure whether they still believed the Christian faith~~ or ~~not.~~

The most common examples of this I saw were the many young adults who had come from more conservative parts of the U.S. to take their undergraduate degrees at a New York City school. Here they met the kind of person they had been warned about for years, those with liberal views on sex, politics, and culture. Despite what they had been led to believe, those peo-

ple were kind, reasonable, and open-hearted. When the students began to experience a change in their own views, they found that many people back home, especially in the churches, responded in a hostile and bigoted way. Soon they had rejected their former views along with their faith. The elder brothers had turned them into younger brothers.

We discovered, however, that younger brothers were willing to come to our church because they saw that we made a clear distinction between the gospel and religious moralism, and that provided an opportunity in which they could explore Christianity from a new perspective.

It is natural for younger brothers to think that elder brotherness and Christianity are exactly the same thing. But Jesus says they are not. In his parable, Jesus deconstructs the religiosity that is one of the main problems with the world. In this parable Jesus says to us, "Would you please be open to the possibility that the gospel, real Christianity, is something very different from religion?" That gives many people hope that

there is a way to know God that doesn't lead to the pathologies of moralism and religiosity.

There is a third group of people who need to understand elder-brother lostness. There is a big difference between an elder brother and a real, gospel-believing Christian. But there are also many genuine Christians who are elder brother*ish.* If you came to Christ out of being a younger brother, there is always the danger of partially relapsing into addictions or other younger-brother sins. But if you've become a Christian out of being an elder brother, you can even more easily slide back into elder-brother attitudes and spiritual deadness. If you have not grasped the gospel fully and deeply, you will return to being condescending, condemning, anxious, insecure, joyless, and angry all the time.

Elder brothers have an undercurrent of anger toward life circumstances, hold grudges long and bitterly, look down at people of other races, religions, and lifestyles, experience life as a joyless, crushing drudgery, have little intimacy and joy in their prayer

lives, and have a deep insecurity that makes them overly sensitive to criticism and rejection yet fierce and merciless in condemning others. What a terrible picture! And yet the rebellious path of the younger brother is obviously not a better alternative.

Most people who follow the philosophy of individual fulfillment and self-discovery do not make a shipwreck of their lives like this younger son. Most religious people who think that God will save them for their moral efforts are not nearly as heartless and angry as this older son. Isn't Jesus exaggerating? The answer is no, he is explaining that while most people do not arrive at these extreme places, each approach to life has the seeds of its own destruction in it, which draws its adherents toward the spiritual destinations he describes so well.

Jesus's parable creates something of a crisis for the thoughtful listener. He has vividly portrayed both of the world's two spiritual paths, the basic ways each offers for finding happiness, relating to God, and dealing with our problems. However, he exposes them

both as profoundly mistaken, as dead ends. He clearly wants us to take some radically different approach, but what is it? Where do we find it?

We will find the answer when we realize that Jesus deliberately left someone out of this parable. He did this so that we would look for him and, finding him, find our own way home at last.

FIVE

✦✧✦

THE TRUE ELDER BROTHER

"My son, everything I have is yours."

What We Need

WHAT do we need to escape the shackles of our particular brand of lostness, whether it be younger-brother or elder-brother? How can the inner dynamic of the heart be changed from one of fear and anger to one of joy, love, and gratitude?

The first thing we need is God's initiating love. Notice how the father comes out to each son and expresses love to him, in order to bring him in. He does not wait for his younger son on the porch of his home, impatiently tapping his foot, murmuring, "Here comes that son of mine. After all he's done, there had better be some real groveling!" There's not

a hint of such an attitude. No, he runs and kisses him before his son can confess. It's not the repentance that causes the father's love, but rather the reverse. The father's lavish affection makes the son's expression of remorse far easier.

The father also goes out to the angry, resentful elder brother, begging him to come into the feast. This picture is like a double-edged sword. It shows that even the most religious and moral people need the initiating grace of God, that they are just as lost; and it shows there is hope, yes, even for Pharisees. This last plea from the father is particularly amazing when we remember Jesus's audience. He is addressing the religious leaders who are going to hand him over to the Roman authorities to be executed. Yet in the story the elder brother gets not a harsh condemnation but a loving plea to turn from his anger and self-righteousness. Jesus is pleading in love with his deadliest enemies.

He is not a Pharisee about Pharisees; he is not self-righteous about self-righteousness. Nor should

(margin handwritten note: What is the son's grief over before the father's forgiveness?)

we be. He not only loves the wild-living, free-spirited people, but also hardened religious people.

We will never find God unless he first seeks us, but we should remember that he can do so in very different ways. Sometimes, God jumps on us dramatically, as he does with the younger son, and we have a sharp sense of his love. Sometimes he quietly and patiently argues with us even though we continue to turn away, as in the case of the older son. How can you tell if he is working on you now? If you begin to sense your lostness and find yourself wanting to escape it, you should realize that that desire is not something you could have generated on your own. Such a process requires Help, and if it is happening it is a good indication that he is even now at your side.

We also learn from this parable that our repentance must go deeper than just regret for individual sins. When the younger brother comes back, he has a long list of wrongdoings for which he must express remorse. When we think of repentance we think, "If you want to get right with God, you get out your list

The degree of drama in the conversion experience is not the test of salvation

of sins and you tell him how sorry you are about each item."

Repentance is not less than that, but it is much more, because the list approach isn't sufficient to address the condition of the elder brother. The older son is lost, outside the feast of the father's love, yet he's got almost nothing on his list of wrongdoings. He says, "I've never disobeyed you," and the father doesn't contradict him, which is Jesus's way of showing us that he is virtually faultless regarding the moral rules. So how does a person who is lost, yet who has no sins on the list, get saved?

Let me be careful to avoid a misunderstanding here. This story is a great metaphor of sin and salvation, but we can't press every single detail literally. Neither Jesus nor any author of the Bible ever implies that any human being is flawless, without sin or fault, except Jesus himself. Instead, the point is that it is a distraction to concentrate only on our specific behavioral shortcomings.

When Pharisees sin they feel terrible and repent.

The True Elder Brother

They may punish themselves and bewail their weakness. When they finish, however, they remain elder brothers. Remorse and regret is just a part of the self-salvation project. Pharisaical repentance doesn't go deep enough to get at the real problem.

What is that problem? Pride in his good deeds, rather than remorse over his bad deeds, was keeping the older son out of the feast of salvation. The elder brother's problem is his self-righteousness, the way he uses his moral record to put God and others in his debt to control them and get them to do what he wants. His spiritual problem is the radical insecurity that comes from basing his self-image on achievements and performance, so he must endlessly prop up his sense of righteousness by putting others down and finding fault. As one of my teachers in seminary put it, the main barrier between Pharisees and God is "not their sins, but their damnable good works."

What must we do, then, to be saved? To find God we must repent of the things we have done wrong, but if that is all you do, you may remain just an elder

brother. ~~To truly become Christians we must also re-pent of the reasons we ever did anything right~~. ~~Phari-sees only repent of their sins, but Christians repent for the very roots of their righteousness, too~~. ~~We must learn how to repent of the sin *under* all our other sins *and* under all our righteousness—the sin of seeking to be our own Savior and Lord~~. We must admit that we've put our ultimate hope and trust in things other than God, and t~~hat in both our wrongdoing and right doing we have been seeking to get around God or get control of God in order to get hold of those things~~.

It is only when you see the desire to be your own Savior and Lord—lying beneath both your sins *and* your moral goodness—that you are on the verge of understanding the gospel and becoming a Christian indeed. When you realize that the antidote to being bad is not just being good, you are on the brink. If you follow through, it will change everything: how you relate to God, self, others, the world, your work, your sins, your virtue. It's called the new birth because it's so radical.

This, however, only brings us to the brink of Jesus's message, not to its heart. This tells us what we must turn from, not what, or whom, we must turn to. We have seen that we need the initiating love of the father, and this deeper, gospel repentance. But there is one more thing we need in order to enter the festival joy of salvation.

Who We Need

Luke 15 informs us in verses 1–3 that Jesus told not one but three parables to the Pharisees who were complaining about his fraternization with sinners. The first parable is called the Parable of the Lost Sheep. A man is tending a flock of one hundred sheep, but one goes astray. Instead of accepting this loss, the shepherd goes out searching until he has found his lost sheep. Then he calls all around to "Rejoice with me, for I have found my lost sheep" (verse 6).

The second parable is called the Parable of the Lost Coin. In this story a woman has ten silver coins in the

house but loses one. She does not write it off as a loss, but instead "lights a lamp, sweeps the whole house, and searches diligently until she finds it" (verse 8). And when she does, she calls her friends and neighbors and says, "Rejoice with me, for I have found my lost coin." The third parable is the story we have been studying, the Parable of the Two Lost Sons.

The similarities among the three stories are obvious. In each parable something is lost—sheep, coin, and son. In each the one who loses something gets it back. And each of the narratives ends on a note of festive rejoicing and celebration when the lost one is returned.

There is, though, one striking difference between the third parable and the first two. In the first two someone "goes out" and searches diligently for that which is lost. The searchers let nothing distract them or stand in their way. By the time we get to the third story, and we hear about the plight of the lost son, we are fully prepared to expect that someone will set out to search for him. No one does. It is startling, and

The True Elder Brother

Jesus meant it to be so. By placing the three parables so closely together, he is inviting thoughtful listeners to ask: "Well, who should have gone out and searched for the lost son?" Jesus knew the Bible thoroughly, and he knew that at its very beginning it tells another story of an elder and younger brother—Cain and Abel. In that story, God tells the resentful and proud older brother: "*You* are your brother's keeper."

Edmund Clowney recounts the true story of a young man who was a U.S. soldier missing in action during the Vietnam War. When the family could get no word of him through any official channel, the older son flew to Vietnam and, risking his life, searched the jungles and the battlefields for his lost brother. It's said that despite the danger, he was never hurt, because those on both sides had heard of his dedication and respected his quest. Some of them called him, simply, "the brother."

This is what the elder brother in the parable should have done; this is what a true elder brother would have done. He would have said, "Father, my younger

brother has been a fool, and now his life is in ruins. ~~But I will go look for him and bring him home. And if the inheritance is gone—as I expect—I'll bring him back into the family at my expen~~se."

Indeed, it is only at the elder brother's expense that the younger brother can be brought back in. Because, as Jesus said, the father had divided his property between them before the younger son had left. Everything had been assigned. The younger brother had gotten his one-third portion and it was completely gone. Now, when the father says to the older brother, "My son, everything I have is yours," he is telling the literal truth. Every penny that remained of the family estate belongs to the elder brother. Every robe, every ring, every fatted calf is his by right.

Over the years many readers have drawn the superficial conclusion that the restoration of the younger brother involved no atonement, no cost. They point out that the younger son wanted to make restitution but the father wouldn't let him—his acceptance back into the family was simply free. This, they say, shows

that forgiveness and love should always be free and unconditional.

That is an oversimplification. If someone breaks your lamp, you could demand that she pay for it. The alternative is that you could forgive her and pay for it yourself (or go about bumping into furniture in the dark). Imagine a more grave situation, namely that someone has seriously damaged your reputation. Again, you have two options. You could make him pay for this by going to others, criticizing and ruining his good name as a way to restore your own. Or you could forgive him, taking on the more difficult task of setting the record straight without vilifying him. The forgiveness is free and unconditional to the perpetrator, but it is costly to you.

Mercy and forgiveness must be free and unmerited to the wrongdoer. If the wrongdoer has to do something to merit it, then it isn't mercy, but forgiveness *always* comes at a cost to the one granting the forgiveness.

While Act 1 of the parable showed us how free

the father's forgiveness is, Act 2 gives us insight into its costliness. The younger brother's restoration was free to him, but it came at enormous cost to the elder brother. The father could not just forgive the younger son, somebody had to pay! The father could not reinstate him except at the expense of the elder brother. There was no other way. But Jesus does not put a true elder brother in the story, one who is willing to pay any cost to seek and save that which is lost. It is heartbreaking. The younger son gets a Pharisee for a brother instead.

But we do not.

By putting a flawed elder brother in the story, Jesus is inviting us to imagine and yearn for a true one.

And we have him. Think of the kind of brother we need. We need one who does not just go to the next country to find us but who will come all the way from heaven to earth. We need one who is willing to pay not just a finite amount of money, but, at the infinite cost of his own life to bring us into God's family, for our debt is so much greater. Either as elder broth-

ers or as younger brothers we have rebelled against the father. We deserve alienation, isolation, and rejection. The point of the parable is that forgiveness always involves a price—someone has to pay. There was no way for the younger brother to return to the family unless the older brother bore the cost himself. Our true elder brother paid our debt, on the cross, in our place.

There Jesus was stripped naked of his robe and dignity so that we could be clothed with a dignity and standing we don't deserve. On the cross Jesus was treated as an outcast so that we could be brought into God's family freely by grace. There Jesus drank the cup of eternal justice so that we might have the cup of the Father's joy. There was no other way for the heavenly Father to bring us in, except at the expense of our true elder brother.

How can the inner workings of the heart be changed from a dynamic of fear and anger to that of love, joy, and gratitude? Here is how. You need to be moved by the sight of what it cost to bring you

home. The key difference between a Pharisee and a believer in Jesus is inner-heart motivation. Pharisees are being good but out of a fear-fueled need to control God. They don't really trust him or love him. To them God is an exacting boss, not a loving father. Christians have seen something that has transformed their hearts toward God so they can finally love and rest in the Father.

The acclaimed foreign film *Three Seasons* is a series of vignettes about life in postwar Vietnam. One of the stories is about a Hai, a cyclo driver (a bicycle rickshaw), and Lan, a beautiful prostitute. Both have deep, unfulfilled desires. Hai is in love with Lan, but she is out of his price range. Lan lives in grinding poverty and longs to live in the beautiful world of the elegant hotels where she works, but in which she never spends the night. She hopes that the money she makes by prostitution will be her means of escape, but instead the work brutalizes and enslaves her.

Then Hai enters a cyclo race and wins the top prize. With the money he brings Lan to the hotel.

He pays for the night and pays her fee. Then, to everyone's shock, he tells her he just wants to watch her fall asleep. Instead of using the power of his wealth to have sex with her, he spends it to purchase a place for her for one night in the normal world, to fulfill her desire to belong. Lan finds such grace deeply troubling at first, thinking Hai has done this to control her. ~~When it becomes apparent that he is using his power to serve rather than use her, it begins to transform her, making it impossible to return to a life of prostitution.~~

Jesus Christ, who had all the power in the world, saw us enslaved by the very things we thought would free us. So he emptied himself of his glory and became a servant (Philippians 2). He laid aside the infinities and immensities of his being and, at the cost of his life, paid the debt for our sins, purchasing us the only place our hearts can rest, in his Father's house.

Knowing he did this will transform us from the inside out, as Hai's selfless love did for Lan. Why wouldn't you want to offer yourself to someone like

this? Selfless love destroys the mistrust in our hearts toward God that makes us either younger brothers *or* elder brothers.

John Newton, the author of the hymn "Amazing Grace," wrote another hymn that puts this perfectly:

> *Our pleasure and our duty,*
> *though opposite before,*
> *since we have seen his beauty*
> *are joined to part no more.*

In a few short words Newton outlines our dilemma. The choice before us seems to be to either turn from God and pursue the desires of our hearts, like the younger brother, or repress desire and do our moral duty, like the older brother. But the sacrificial, costly love of Jesus on the cross changes that. When we see the beauty of what he has done for us, it attracts our hearts to him. We realize that the love, the greatness, the consolation, and the honor we have been seeking in other things is here. The beauty also eliminates our

fear. If the Lord of the Universe loves us enough to experience this for us, what are we afraid of? To the degree we "see his beauty" we will be free from the fear and neediness that creates either younger brothers or elder brothers.

John Newton's friend, the poet William Cowper, treats this idea in another hymn:

> *To see the Law by Christ fulfilled,*
> *and hear his pardoning voice,*
> *changes a slave into a child*
> *and duty into choice.*

We will never stop being younger brothers or elder brothers until we acknowledge our need, rest by faith, and gaze in wonder at the work of our true elder brother, Jesus Christ.

SIX

REDEFINING HOPE

"He set off for a far country."

Our Longing for Home

IT is important to read Jesus's parable of the lost son in the context of the whole of Luke, chapter 15, but the story has an even larger context. If we read the narrative in light of the Bible's sweeping theme of exile and homecoming we will understand that Jesus has given us more than a moving account of individual redemption. He has retold the story of the whole human race, and promised nothing less than hope for the world.

In Jesus's parable the younger brother goes off into a distant country expecting a better life but is disappointed. He begins to long for home, remembering the food in his father's house. So do we all.

Redefining Hope

"Home" exercises a powerful influence over human life. Foreign-born Americans spend billions annually to visit the communities in which they were born. Children who never find a place where they feel they belong carry an incapacity for attachment into their adult lives. Many of us have fond memories of times, people, and places where we felt we were truly home. However, if we ever have an opportunity to get back to the places we remember so fondly, we are usually disappointed. For thirty-nine years my wife, Kathy, spent summers with her family in a ramshackle cottage on the shores of Lake Erie. The very memory of that place is nourishing to Kathy's spirit. But returning to the actual, now-dilapidated property is a gut-wrenching experience. It won't be much different if someone buys it and puts up new condos on it. An actual visit to the place will always present her with a sense of loss.

Home, then, is a powerful but elusive concept. The strong feelings that surround it reveal some deep longing within us for a place that absolutely fits and

suits us, where we can be, or perhaps find, our true selves. Yet it seems that no real place or actual family ever satisfies these yearnings, though many situations arouse them. In his novel a *A Separate Peace,* John Knowles's central character discovers that summer mornings in New Hampshire give him "some feeling so hopelessly promising that I would fall back in my bed to guard against it . . . I wanted to break out crying from stabs of hopeless joy, or intolerable promise, or because those mornings were too full of beauty for me." In *East of Eden,* John Steinbeck similarly says of the mountains of central California that he wanted "to climb into their warm foothills almost as you want to climb into the lap of a beloved mother."[11]

The memory of home seems to be powerfully evoked by certain sights, sounds, and even smells. But they can only arouse a desire they can't fulfill. Many of the people in my church have shared with me how disappointing Christmas and Thanksgiving are to them. They prepare for holidays hoping that, finally, this year, the gathering of the family at that important

place will deliver the experience of warmth, joy, comfort, and love that they want from it. But these events almost always fail, crushed under the weight of our impossible expectations.

There is a German word that gets at this concept— the word *Sehnsucht*. Dictionaries will tell you that there is no simple English synonym. It denotes profound homesickness or longing, but with transcendent overtones. The writer who spoke most of this "spiritual homesickness" was C. S. Lewis, in his famous sermon "The Weight of Glory." He refers to many similar experiences like those described by Steinbeck and Knowles, and then he says:

> Our commonest expedient is to call it beauty and behave as if that had settled the matter. Wordsworth's expedient was to identify it with certain moments in his own past. But all this is a cheat. If Wordsworth had gone back to those moments in the past, he would not have found the thing itself, but only the reminder of it; what

he remembered would turn out to be itself a remembering. The books or the music in which
we thought the beauty was located will betray
us if we trust to them; it was not in them, it only
came through them, and what came through
them was longing. These things—the beauty,
the memory of our own past—are good images
of what we really desire; but if they are mistaken for the thing itself they turn into dumb
idols, breaking the hearts of their worshippers.
For they are not the thing itself. . . . Now we
wake to find . . . [w]e have been mere specta-
tors. Beauty has smiled, but not to welcome us;
her face was turned in our direction, but not to
see us. We have not been accepted, welcomed,
or taken in. . . .

Our life-long nostalgia, our longing to be reunited with something in the universe from
which we feel cut off, to be on the inside of
some door which we have always seen from the

Redefining Hope

outside, is no mere neurotic fancy, but the truest index of our real situation.[12]

There seems to be a sense, then, in which we are all like the younger brother. We are all exiles, always longing for home. We are always traveling, never arriving. The houses and families we actually inhabit are only inns along the way, but they aren't home. Home continues to evade us.

Why would "home" be so powerful and yet so elusive for us? The answer can be found as we examine one of the most pervasive themes of the Bible. The experience we have been describing is the trace in our souls of this larger story.

In the beginning of the book of Genesis we learn the reason why all people feel like exiles, like we aren't really home. We are told there that we were created to live in the garden of God. That was the world we were built for, a place in which there was no parting from love, no decay or disease. It was all these things because it was life before the face of God, in his pres-

ence. There we were to adore and serve his infinite majesty, and to know, enjoy, and reflect his infinite beauty. That was our original home, the true country we were made for.

However, the Bible teaches that, as in Jesus's parable, God was the "father" of that home and we chafed under his authority. We wanted to live without God's interference, and so we turned away, and became alienated from him, and lost our home for the same reason the younger brother lost his. The result was exile.

The Bible says that we have been wandering as spiritual exiles ever since. That is, we have been living in a world that no longer fits our deepest longings. Though we long for bodies that "run and are not weary," we have become subject to disease, aging, and death. Though we need love that lasts, all our relationships are subject to the inevitable entropy of time, and they crumble in our hands. Even people who stay true to us die and leave us, or we die and leave them. Though we long to make a difference in the world

through our work, we experience endless frustration. We never fully realize our hopes and dreams. We may work hard to re-create the home that we have lost, but, says the Bible, it only exists in the presence of the heavenly father from which we have fled.

This theme is played out again and again in the Bible. After Adam and Eve's exile from the ultimate home, their son Cain was forced to restlessly wander the earth because he murdered his brother Abel. Later Jacob cheated his father and brother and fled into exile for years. After that, Jacob's son Joseph and his family were taken from their homeland into Egypt because of a famine. There the Israelites were enslaved until, under Moses, they returned to their ancestral home. Centuries after this, David, before he became king, lived as a hunted fugitive. Finally the whole nation of Israel was exiled again, taken captive to Babylon by King Nebuchadnezzar.

It is no coincidence that story after story contains the pattern of exile. The message of the Bible is that the human race is a band of exiles trying to come

home. The parable of the prodigal son is about every one of us.

The Difficulty of Return

"Home," Robert Frost famously said, "is where, when you have to go there, they have to take you in" ("The Death of the Hired Man"). The younger brother, however, knows that a successful return is not inevitable. Why? His sins have created a barrier and he does not know how that wall can be breached. He knows he might be rejected and forced to stay in exile. In the same way, the Bible shows how high the barriers are for our own homecoming as a human race.

During the Babylonian exile, the prophets of Israel predicted a great return and homecoming through the grace of God. Eventually the people of Israel were given permission to leave Babylon and return to their homeland. Only a minority of the Jews actually returned to Palestine, and there they continued

Redefining Hope

to be under the domination of Persia. Then one great world power after another invaded and controlled Israel, first Greece, then Syria, and finally Rome.

The people were still oppressed. All the mini-exoduses and mini-homecomings of the Bible failed in the end to deliver the final and full homecoming the prophets promised and everyone longed for. Why? One reason was the brokenness *within* human beings. Israel in particular and the human race in general was still mired in selfishness, pride, and sin. We are oppressed by conflicts within our own hearts as well as by constant battles and warfare with neighboring nations. We need a radical change in our very nature.

The second reason is the brokenness *around* human beings. There is more to the state of "exile" than just human moral evil. According to the Bible, we live in a natural world that is now fallen. We were not made for a world of disease and natural disaster, a world in which everything decays and dies, including ourselves. This world, as it now exists, is not the home we long for. A real, final homecoming would

mean a radical change not only in human nature but in the very fabric of the material world. How can such a thing be accomplished?

By the time of Jesus's ministry, many in Israel realized that despite the return from Babylon, the nation was still in exile. Injustice and oppression, loss and affliction still dominated national life. The final homecoming had not yet happened. Many, therefore, began to pray to God for it, but they conceived of it as a national, political liberation for Israel. It was thought that the Messiah, the king who would redeem Israel, would be a figure of great military strength and political power. He would come to his people, be recognized and received by them, and then lead them on to victory.

Then Jesus appeared, and declared that he was bringing in "the kingdom of God" (Mark 1:15). The people crowded eagerly around to observe and hear him, but nothing about him fit their expectations. He was born not in a palace behind a royal curtain, but in a stable feed trough, on the straw, far from home.

Redefining Hope

During his ministry he wandered, settling nowhere, and said: "Foxes have holes, and birds have nests, but the Son of Man has nowhere to lay his head" (Matthew 8:20). He remained completely outside the social networks of political and economic power. He did not even seek academic or religious credentials. Finally, at the end of his life, he was crucified outside the gate of the city, a powerful symbol of rejection by the community, of exile. And as he died he said, "My God, my God, why have you forsaken me?" (Matthew 27:46), a tremendous cry of spiritual dereliction and homelessness.

What had happened? Jesus had not come to simply deliver one nation from political oppression, but to save all of us from sin, evil, and death itself. He came to bring the human race Home. Therefore he did not come in strength but in weakness. He came and experienced the exile that we deserved. He was expelled from the presence of the Father, he was thrust into the darkness, the uttermost despair of spiritual alienation—in our place. He took upon himself the

full curse of human rebellion, cosmic homelessness, so that we could be welcomed into our true home.

The Feast at the End of History

Jesus not only died, but rose from the grave on the third day. He broke the power of death (Hebrews 2:14): "But God raised him from the dead, freeing him from the agony of death, because it was impossible for death to keep its hold on him" (Acts 2:24). Because Jesus paid the penalty for our sin with his death, he has achieved victory over the forces of death, decay, and disorder that keep the world from being our true home. Someday he will return to make this victory complete. Isaiah writes:

"Your God will come . . . he will come to save you. Then will the eyes of the blind be opened and the ears of the deaf be unstopped. Then will the lame leap like a deer, and the mute tongue shout for joy. The ransomed of the Lord will

return, they will enter Zion with singing. Everlasting joy will crown their heads. Gladness and joy will overtake them, and sorrow and sighing will flee away." (Isaiah 35)

At the end of the story of the prodigal sons, there is a feast of homecoming. So too at the end of the book of Revelation, at the end of history, there is a feast, the "marriage supper of the Lamb" (Revelation 19). The Lamb is Jesus, who was sacrificed for the sins of the world so that we could be pardoned and brought home. This feast happens in the New Jerusalem, the City of God that comes down out of heaven to fill the earth (Revelation 21–22). We are told that the very presence of God is in this city, and so is, remarkably, the tree of life, whose leaves now effect "the healing of the nations" (Revelation 22:2). The tree of life, of course, was in the Garden of Eden. At the end of history the whole earth has become the Garden of God again. Death and decay and suffering are gone. The nations are no longer at war. "He will wipe every

tear from their eyes. There will be no more death or mourning or crying or pain—for the old order of things has passed away" (Revelation 21:4).

Jesus, unlike the founder of any other major faith, holds out hope for ordinary human life. Our future is not an ethereal, impersonal form of consciousness. We will not float through the air, but rather will eat, embrace, sing, laugh, and dance in the kingdom of God, in degrees of power, glory, and joy that we can't at present imagine.

Jesus will make the world our perfect home again. We will no longer be living "east of Eden," always wandering and never arriving. We will come, and the father will meet us and embrace us, and we will be brought into the feast.

SEVEN

THE FEAST OF THE FATHER

"He heard music and dancing."

I F we believe the gospel, rest in Jesus's work, and receive a new identity and relationship with God, what then? How will our lives change as we live them based on Jesus's message about sin, grace, and hope?

In Isaiah's predictions of the new heavens and new earth, he declares that, like all homecomings, this final one will be marked by the ultimate party-feast (Isaiah 25). Jesus, too, constantly depicts the salvation he brings as a feast. "Many will come from the east and the west," he said to his followers, "and will take their places at the feast with Abraham, Isaac and Jacob in the kingdom of heaven" (Matthew 8:11). He left a meal—what we today call the Lord's Sup-

per or Eucharist—as a sign of his saving grace. And, of course, Jesus's parable of the lost sons ends in a party-feast that represents the great festival of God at the end of history.

Why does he speak this way? He does so because there is no better way to convey vividly what it means to live out a life based on his saving work. There are four ways to experience a feast that correspond to the ways our lives will be shaped by Jesus's gospel message.

Salvation Is Experiential

A feast is a place where our appetites and our senses—of sight, smell, sound, and taste—are filled up. In John 2, we are told that Jesus was in attendance at a wedding reception where the wine had run out too early. Both the bridal couple and "the master of the banquet," what we might call the master of ceremonies, were in danger of social humiliation. However, in his first public exercise of divine power, Jesus turned sev-

eral large containers of water into wine. Amazingly, John the gospel writer calls this miracle a "sign," a signifier of what Jesus's ministry was all about. Why would this be his inaugural act? Why would Jesus, to convey what he had come to do, choose to turn 150 gallons of water into superb wine in order to keep a party going?

The answer is that Jesus came to bring festival joy. He is the real, the true "Master of the Banquet," the Lord of the Feast. As we have seen, Jesus took the penalty for our sin for us, in our place. Christian theologians have therefore spoken about the law-court aspect of Jesus's salvation. Jesus secures the legal verdict "not guilty" for us so we are no longer liable for our wrongdoings. However, salvation is not only objective and legal but also subjective and experiential. The Bible insists on using sensory language about salvation. It calls us to "taste and see" that the Lord is good, not only to agree and believe it. In his famous sermon, "A Divine and Supernatural Light," Jonathan Edwards said:

"There is a difference between believing that God is holy and gracious, and having a new sense on the heart of the loveliness and beauty of that holiness and grace. The difference between believing that God is gracious and tasting that God is gracious is as different as having a rational belief that honey is sweet and having the actual sense of its sweetness."[13]

Jesus's salvation is a feast, and therefore when we believe in and rest in his work for us, through the Holy Spirit he becomes real to our hearts. His love is like honey, or like wine. Rather than only believing that he is loving, we can come to sense the reality, the beauty, and the power of his love. His love can become more real to you than the love of anyone else. It can delight, galvanize, and console you. That will lift you up and free you from fear like nothing else.

This makes all the difference. If you are filled with shame and guilt, you do not merely need to believe in the abstract concept of God's mercy. You must sense,

on the palate of the heart, as it were, the sweetness of his mercy. Then you will know you are accepted. If you are filled with worry and anxiety, you do not only need to believe that God is in control of history. You must see, with eyes of the heart, his dazzling majesty. Then you will know he has things in hand.

Is it really possible to have this kind of experience? Some people find this more difficult than others, because they are of a more rational, controlled temperament. Other people, I believe, are so hungry for mystical experiences that they read every intuition and strong feeling as a "word from the Lord." In short, most of us are too eager or not eager enough for what Jesus offers. But he does offer access to the presence of the Father. It is only a foretaste now, and it waxes and wanes over the years as we pray and seek his face with the help of the Spirit. But it is available. The hymn writer Isaac Watts speaks of it in these lines: "The hill of Zion yields a thousand sacred sweets *before* we reach the heavenly fields or walk the golden streets."

Salvation Is Material

A meal is a very physical experience. Jesus left a meal, the Lord's Supper, to be remembered by, and the final goal of history is a meal, the wedding supper of the Lamb (Revelation 19). The resurrected Christ ate with his disciples when he met with them (Luke 24:42–43; John 21:9). What does it all mean? It is a sign that, for Jesus, this material world matters.

The book of Genesis tells us that when God made this world he looked upon the physical creation and called it "good." He loves and cares for the material world. The fact of Jesus's resurrection and the promise of a new heavens and new earth show clearly that he still cares for it. This world is not simply a theater for individual conversion narratives, to be discarded at the end when we all go to heaven. No, the ultimate purpose of Jesus is not only individual salvation and pardon for sins but also the renewal of this world, the end of disease, poverty, injustice, violence, suffering, and death. The climax of history is not a higher form

of disembodied consciousness but a feast. God made the world with all its colors, tastes, lights, sounds, with all its life-forms living in interdependent systems. It is now marred, stained, and broken, and he will not rest until he has put it right.

If the material world were only an illusion, as Eastern philosophy says, or only a temporary copy of the real, ideal world, as Plato says, then what happens in this world or in this life would be unimportant. All that would matter would be issues of soul or spirit. However, Jesus was not simply saved "in spirit" but was resurrected in body. God has made both soul and body and is going to redeem both soul and body. Everything about the ministry of Jesus demonstrated this fact. Jesus not only preached the word, but also healed the sick, fed the hungry, and cared for the needs of the poor.

In Matthew 25, Jesus describes Judgment Day. Many will stand there and call him "Lord," but Jesus says, stunningly, that if they had not been serving the hungry, the refugee, the sick, and the prisoner, then

they hadn't been serving him (Matthew 25:34–40). This is no contradiction to what we have heard from Jesus in the Parable of the Prodigal Son. He is not saying that only the social workers get into heaven. Rather, he is saying that the inevitable sign that you know you are a sinner saved by sheer, costly grace is a sensitive social conscience and a life poured out in deeds of service to the poor. Younger brothers are too selfish and elder brothers are too self-righteous to care for the poor.

Christianity, therefore, is perhaps the most materialistic of the world's faiths. Jesus's miracles were not so much violations of the natural order, but a restoration of the natural order. God did not create a world with blindness, leprosy, hunger, and death in it. Jesus's miracles were signs that someday all these corruptions of his creation would be abolished. Christians therefore can talk of saving the soul and of building social systems that deliver safe streets and warm homes in the same sentence. With integrity.

Jesus hates suffering, injustice, evil, and death so

much, he came and experienced it to defeat it and, someday, to wipe the world clean of it. Knowing all this, Christians cannot be passive about hunger, sickness, and injustice. Karl Marx and others have charged that religion is "the opiate of the masses." That is, it is a sedative that makes people passive toward injustice, because there will be "pie in the sky bye and bye." That may be true of some religions that teach people that this material world is unimportant or illusory. Christianity, however, teaches that God hates the suffering and oppression of this material world so much, he was willing to get involved in it and to fight against it. Properly understood, Christianity is by no means the opiate of the people. It's more like the smelling salts.

Salvation Is Individual

A meal fuels growth through nourishment. The Lord's Supper, also called Communion or the Eucharist, represents ongoing growth in God's grace. In order

to survive and grow, individuals must eat and drink regularly. That's what we must do with the gospel of the grace of God. We must personally appropriate it, making it more and more central to everything we see, think, and feel. That is how we grow spiritually in wisdom, love, joy, and peace.

Religion operates on the principle of "I obey—therefore I am accepted by God." The basic operating principle of the gospel is "I am accepted by God through the work of Jesus Christ—therefore I obey." As we have seen, believing the gospel is how a person first makes a connection to God. It gives us a new relationship with God and a new identity. We must not think, however, that once believing it, the Christian is now finished with the gospel message. A fundamental insight of Martin Luther's was that "religion" is the default mode of the human heart. Your computer operates automatically in a default mode unless you deliberately tell it to do something else. So Luther says that even after you are converted by the gospel your heart will go back to operating on other

principles unless you deliberately, repeatedly set it to gospel-mode.

We habitually and instinctively look to other things besides God and his grace as our justification, hope, significance, and security. We believe the gospel at one level, but at deeper levels we do not. Human approval, professional success, power and influence, family and clan identity—all of these things serve as our heart's "functional trust" rather than what Christ has done, and as a result we continue to be driven to a great degree by fear, anger, and a lack of self-control. You cannot change such things through mere will-power, through learning Biblical principles and trying to carry them out. We can only change permanently as we take the gospel more deeply into our under-standing and into our hearts. We must feed on the gospel, as it were, digesting it and making it part of ourselves. That is how we grow.

How does this work?

It manifests itself in many ways. You may wish to become more generous with your money. This will

not happen by simply putting pressure on your will to do so. Instead, you should reflect on the things that are holding you back from more radical giving. For many of us, having a lot of money is a way we can get others' approval and respect, and a way of feeling we have control of our lives. Money comes to be not just a thing, but something our heart puts its hope and trust in. Look at how St. Paul, in his letter to the Corinthian church, helped them grow in the grace of generosity. He doesn't put pressure directly on the will, saying, "I'm an apostle and this is your duty to me," nor pressure directly on the emotions, telling them stories about how much the poor are suffering and how much more they have than the sufferers. Instead, he says, "You know the grace of our Lord Jesus Christ, that though he was rich, yet for your sakes he became poor, so that you through his poverty might become rich" (2 Corinthians 8:9). Paul is taking them back to the gospel. He is saying, "Think on his costly grace—until you want to give like he did."

You may wish to strengthen your marriage. In

The Feast of the Father

Ephesians 5, Paul is speaking to spouses but especially to husbands. Many of Paul's readers had brought bad attitudes into their marriages from their pagan backgrounds. Marriage in the dominant society was seen as mainly a business transaction—you needed to marry as "well" as you could for social and economic standing. Sexual gratification was looked for elsewhere. Also, men were taught to despise women and not relate to them as peers or as friends. Paul, however, wants to encourage husbands to be not only sexually faithful but also to cherish and honor their wives, and to help them grow personally and spiritually. That was a wholly new attitude toward marriage.

But notice how Paul goes about motivating his readers. Again, Paul does not threaten or merely exhort, nor does he lift up some shining example to emulate. Instead he vividly portrays the salvation of Jesus as sacrificial, spousal love. "Husbands, love your wives just as Christ loved the church and gave himself up for her . . . to present her to himself as a radiant church, without stain or wrinkle or any other blemish." Jesus

doesn't love us because we are beautiful; we become beautiful through Jesus's sacrificial love. He is the ultimate spouse to us, his "bride," in the gospel.

The solution to stinginess is a reorientation to the generosity of Christ in the gospel, where he poured out his wealth for you. You don't have to worry about money, for the cross proves God's care for you and gives you all the security you need. Jesus's love and salvation confers on you a remarkable status—one that money cannot give you. The solution to a bad marriage is a reorientation to the radical spousal love of Christ in the gospel. "Thou shalt not commit adultery" makes sense in the context of the spousal love of Jesus, especially in the cross, where he was completely faithful to you. Only when you know the spousal love of Christ will you have real fortitude against lust. His love is fulfilling—which keeps you from looking to sexuality to give you what only Jesus can give.

What is the point? What makes you faithful or generous is not just a redoubled effort to follow moral rules. Rather, all change comes from deepen-

ing your understanding of the salvation of Christ and living out of the changes that understanding creates in your heart. Faith in the gospel restructures our motivations, our self-understanding, our identity, and our view of the world. Behavioral compliance to rules without heart-change will be superficial and fleeting.

The gospel is therefore not just the ABCs of the Christian life, but the A to Z of the Christian life. Our problems arise largely because we don't continually return to the gospel to work it in and live it out. That is why Martin Luther wrote, "The truth of the Gospel is the principle article of all Christian doctrine. . . . Most necessary is it that we know this article well, teach it to others, and beat it into their heads continually."[14]

"Wait," I have heard people object. "You mean that in order to grow in Christ, you keep telling yourself how graciously loved and accepted you are? That doesn't seem to be the best way to make progress. Maybe the motivation of religion was negative, but

at least it was effective! You knew you *had* to obey God because if you didn't, he wouldn't answer your prayers or take you to heaven. But if you remove this fear and talk so much about free grace and unmerited acceptance—what incentive will you have to live a good life? It seems like this gospel way of living won't produce people who are as faithful and diligent to obey God's will without question."

But if, when you have lost all fear of punishment you also have lost incentive to live an obedient life, then what was your motivation in the first place? It could only have been fear. What other incentive is there? Awed, grateful love.

Some years ago I met a woman who began coming to Redeemer, the church where I am a minister. She said that she had gone to a church growing up and she had always heard that God accepts us only if we are sufficiently good and ethical. She had never heard the message she was now hearing, that we can be accepted by God by sheer grace through the work of Christ regardless of anything we do or have done.

The Feast of the Father

She said, "*That* is a scary idea! Oh, it's good scary, but still scary."

I was intrigued. I asked her what was so scary about unmerited free grace? She replied something like this: "If I was saved by my good works—then there would be a limit to what God could ask of me or put me through. I would be like a taxpayer with rights. I would have done my duty and now I would deserve a certain quality of life. But if it is really true that I am a sinner saved by sheer grace—at God's infinite cost—then there's nothing he cannot ask of me." She could see immediately that the wonderful-beyond-belief teaching of salvation by sheer grace had two edges to it. On the one hand it cut away slavish fear. God loves us freely, despite our flaws and failures. Yet she also knew that if Jesus really had done this for her—she was not her own. She was bought with a price.

Over the years I have heard many people say, "Well, if I believed that I was saved by sheer grace, not because of my good works, then I could live any

way I wanted!" But this is to live as if Jesus's parable had only an Act 1, and not an Act 2. God's grace is free, yes, but it is also costly, infinitely so. Dietrich Bonhoeffer was appalled at how many in the German church capitulated to Hitler in the early 1930s, and in response he wrote his great work *The Cost of Discipleship*. There he warned about the dangers of what he called "cheap grace," the teaching that stresses only that grace is free, so it doesn't really matter how we live. The solution, he said, was not to return to legalism, but to focus on how seriously God takes sin and on how he could only save us from it at infinite cost to himself. Understanding this must and will profoundly reshape our lives. We will not be able to live in a selfish, cowardly way. We will stand up for justice and sacrifice for our neighbor. And we won't mind the cost of following after Christ when we compare it to the price he paid to rescue us.

A Biblical text that conveys this is Jesus's parable of the sower in Matthew 13. The preacher of God's word, the gospel, is likened to a sower of seed. There

are three groups of people who "receive" and accept the gospel, but two of the groups do not produce changed lives. One set of people do not have the endurance and patience to handle suffering, while another group continues to live an anxious, materialistic life. The only group of people who produce changed lives are not those who have worked harder or been more obedient, but those who "hear the word of God and *understand* it" (Matthew 13:23). Bonhoeffer insisted that people whose lives remained unchanged by God's grace didn't really understand its costliness, and therefore didn't really understand the gospel. They had a general idea of God's universal love, but not a real grasp of the seriousness of sin and the meaning of Christ's work on our behalf.

In the end, Martin Luther's old formula still sums things up nicely: "We are saved by faith alone [not our works], but not by faith that remains alone." Nothing we do can merit God's grace and favor, we can only believe that he has given it to us in Jesus Christ and receive it by faith. But if we truly believe and trust in

the one who sacrificially served us, it changes us into people who sacrificially serve God and our neighbors. If we say "I believe in Jesus" but it doesn't affect the way we live, the answer is not that now we need to add hard work to our faith so much as that we haven't truly understood or believed in Jesus at all.

Salvation Is Communal

Feasting is communal by nature. No reunion, family gathering, wedding, or other significant social event is complete without a meal. When we invite someone to eat with us, it is an invitation to relax a bit and get to know one another. In many cultures, to offer to eat with someone is to offer them friendship.

We live in a culture in which the interests and desires of the individual take precedence over those of the family, group, or community. As a result, a high percentage of people want to achieve spiritual growth without losing their independence to a church or to any organized institution. This is often the meaning

behind the common protestations "I am spiritual, but not religious" and "I like Jesus, but not Christianity." Many people who are spiritually searching have had bad experiences with churches. So they want nothing further to do with them. They are interested in a relationship with God, but not if they have to be part of an organization.

I have explained in this book why churches—and all religious institutions—are often so unpleasant. They are filled with elder brothers. Yet staying away from them simply because they have elder brothers is just another form of self-righteousness. Besides that, there is no way you will be able to grow spiritually apart from a deep involvement in a community of other believers. You can't live the Christian life without a band of Christian friends, without a family of believers in which you find a place.

C. S. Lewis was part of a famous circle of friends called the Inklings, which included J. R. R. Tolkien, the author of *The Lord of the Rings,* and also the author Charles Williams, who died unexpectedly after

World War II. In his book *The Four Loves,* Lewis wrote a striking meditation on his death in an essay entitled "Friendship."

> In each of my friends there is something that only some other friend can fully bring out. By myself I am not large enough to call the whole man into activity; I want other lights than my own to show all his facets. Now that Charles [Williams] is dead, I shall never again see Ronald's [Tolkien's] reaction to a specifically Charles joke. Far from having more of Ronald, having him "to myself" now that Charles is away, I have less of Ronald . . . In this, Friendship exhibits a glorious "nearness by resemblance" to heaven itself where the very multitude of the blessed (which no man can number) increases the fruition which each of us has of God. For every soul, seeing Him in her own way, doubtless communicates that unique vision to all the rest. That, says an old author, is why the Sera-

phim in Isaiah's vision are crying "Holy, Holy, Holy" to one another (Isaiah 6:3). The more we thus share the Heavenly Bread between us, the more we shall have.[15]

Lewis is saying that it took a community to know an individual. How much more would this be true of Jesus Christ? Christians commonly say they want a relationship with Jesus, that they want to "get to know Jesus better." You will never be able to do that by yourself. You must be deeply involved in the church, in Christian community, with strong relationships of love and accountability. Only if you are part of a community of believers seeking to resemble, serve, and love Jesus will you ever get to know him and grow into his likeness.

Babette's Feast

Jesus's great Parable of the Prodigal Son retells the story of the entire Bible and the story of the human

race. Within the story, Jesus teaches that the two most common ways to live are both spiritual dead ends. He shows how the plotlines of our lives can only find a resolution, a happy ending, in him, in his person and work.

Isak Dinesen's beloved story "Babette's Feast" also ends with a feast, and also teaches us about two common ways to live that are inadequate, and the reality of another path.

Dinesen's story is about two elderly women, Martine and Phillipa, the daughters of a very strict pastor who had founded a small religious sect in their village. Growing up, both women had been tempted to live a life of sensuality. Martine was wooed by a dashing young lieutenant who wanted to whisk her away. Phillipa was sought after by the director of the Paris Opera, who was entranced by the purity and clarity of her voice. Both women ultimately turned away from a life of worldly pleasure to assist their father in his mission. After he died, the women continued to preside

over the strict religious and moral community in a small village on the bleak coast of Jutland, in western Denmark.

But the community did not fare well. The people's lives became as cold and barren as the wet, gray, windy weather of the region. Nearly everyone had a falling-out with someone else in the town. Many were not speaking to one another. Pride and grievances had been nursed, and bitterness had grown to painful proportions. The village was an utterly joyless place.

Then Martine and Phillipa took in a political refugee, Babette, who lived with them as a servant. When Babette unexpectedly won the lottery, she offered to pay for and prepare an anniversary dinner for the community in honor of their father's birthday. It turned out that Babette had been one of the greatest chefs of Paris, and the meal she planned was a gourmet feast.

The day of the meal came and the guests arrived. An elderly woman who lived near the village, Mrs. Loewenholm, wanted to honor the memory of the pastor, and so invited her nephew to join her at the

dinner. The nephew was none other than Martine's young dashing lieutenant from many years ago, now a great general. As the general arrived in the carriage, he mused upon the past. He felt that for all his worldly success he had not achieved happiness. He remembered Martine and her spiritual seriousness and wondered if he had missed out on what really mattered in life. Martine and Phillipa, however, had not achieved what they had hoped for, either, though they had followed the path of religious service.

Everyone then sat down and began to eat. They were immediately astonished at the exquisite quality and perfect preparation of the food. The power of the feast began to break through the defenses of the people. One by one, under the influence of wonderful food and drink, former enemies began to soften toward one another. Comments and words as sweet as the food began to pass between them. Forgiveness was sought and granted. Two women who had not spoken with each other for many years now touched foreheads affectionately, saying, "God bless you, dear

Solveig" and "God bless you, too, dear Anna." Finally Phillipa began to sing with her pure and beautiful voice and everyone listened, and remembered.

Then the general rose to speak. He quoted Psalm 85: "For mercy and truth have met together and righteousness and bliss have kissed one another." He then said that during this meal he had come to realize that, somehow, morality and joy, the ethical and the sensual, can come together.

Isak Dinesen resolves the story lines nicely. The villagers experience a healing of community. Babette, too, is transformed. She had felt like an outsider in the village, but now she was home, no longer a refugee. Even the general leaves without the regrets with which he had come.

Nevertheless the story does not provide us with a clear answer to the chief question it poses so well. Both the worldly life of sensual pleasure and the religious life of ethical strictness fail to give the human heart what it is seeking. Kierkegaard, the great Danish philosopher who influenced Isak Dinesen, called these

two ways the "aesthetic" and the "ethical," and in his writings he shows that neither approach to life is adequate. But what is the alternative? At Babette's feast, the diners have the momentary mystical experience in which these two things—"righteousness and bliss"—meet. Dinesen is professing her belief that something exists beyond these two alternatives, something that is neither the selfishness of the "aesthetic" nor the severity of the "ethical." She couldn't find a better way of representing that something than a wonderful meal, a great feast.

Jesus's parable answers the question that Dinesen's story poses so skillfully. Jesus says, "I am the Bread of Heaven." Jesus tells us that both the sensual way of the younger brother and the ethical way of the elder brother are spiritual dead ends. He also shows us there is another way: through him. And to enter that way and to live a life based on his salvation will bring us finally to the ultimate party and feast at the end of history. We can have a foretaste of that future salvation now in all the ways outlined in this chapter: in prayer,

in service to others, in the changes in our inner nature through the gospel, and through the healed relationships that Christ can give us now. But they are only a foretaste of what is to come.

On this mountain the LORD Almighty will prepare
  a feast of rich food for all peoples,
  a banquet of aged wine—
  the best of meats and the finest of wines.
On this mountain he will destroy
  the shroud that enfolds all peoples,
  the sheet that covers all nations;
  he will swallow up death forever.
The Sovereign LORD will wipe away the tears
  from all faces;
  he will remove the disgrace of his people
  from all the earth.
The LORD has spoken. (Isaiah 25:6–8)

Acknowledgments

I AM again thankful to Jill Lamar, David McCormick, and Brian Tart, whose literary skill and personal support made this book possible. As always, thanks to Janice Worth and Lynn Land, who make it possible for me to study and write in peace for two weeks each summer. I also thank the people of Redeemer Presbyterian Church, who opened their minds and hearts to the counterintuitive message of this book.

Years ago I heard Dr. Ed Clowney preach on the parable of the prodigal son, and it changed my whole way of thinking about Christianity and how to communicate it. As I got to know him over the years he also taught me that it was possible to be theologically

Acknowledgments

sound and completely orthodox and yet unfailingly gracious—a rare and precious combination.

If I were to make a list of all the men and women who have mentored and encouraged me, as well as shaped my ministry, it would be many pages long. However, the list would have to include: Barbara Boyd, Richard Lovelace, Roger Nicole, R. C. Sproul, Elisabeth Elliot, Kennedy Smartt, Harvie Conn, Jack Miller and, as always, my wife, Kathy. My deepest gratitude.

Tim Keller
June, 2008

Notes

Introduction

1. The sermon has been published under the title "Sharing the Father's Welcome" in his volume *Preaching Christ from All of Scripture* (Crossway, 2003). For three years I jointly taught a graduate course on preaching with Dr. Clowney. During that time I shared with him how I had built upon his foundation and what I believed were the radical implications of this parable of Jesus. He was highly affirming of the material, which is now in this book.

2. I have consulted many other commentaries and studies on Luke's fifteenth chapter but I want to acknowledge a special debt to the work by Kenneth E. Bailey, *Finding the Lost Cultural Keys to Luke 15* (Concordia, 1992) for many of the insights into the parable's

cultural and historical backgrounds that I use in this volume.

ONE—The People Around Jesus

3. J. R. R. Tolkien, *The Two Towers* (Harper Collins, 2004), p. 577.

4. This dialogue is based on an illustration from a sermon by Richard Lucas of St. Helen's Bishopsgate Anglican Church, London, UK.

THREE—Redefining Sin

5. The screenplay for *Witness,* by Earl W. Wallace and William Kelley, can be found at www.harrisonford-web.com/Multimedia/witness.pdf (accessed on December 31, 2007).

6. Flannery O'Connor, *Wise Blood: A Novel* (Farrar, Straus, and Giroux, 1990), p. 22.

7. The script for Peter Shaffer's play *Amadeus* can be found at http://www.imsdb.com/scripts/Amadeus .html (accessed on December 30, 2007).

8. In Luke 18 Jesus tells the parable of a tax collector (a collaborator with the Roman occupational forces)

Notes

and a Pharisee. The Pharisee is very moral and upright but self-satisfied, while the tax collector is a moral failure, but repentant. Jesus concludes: "I tell you that this man [the tax collector], rather than the other, went home justified before God. For everyone who exalts himself will be humbled, and he who humbles himself will be exalted" (Luke 18:14). Compare also Jesus's words to the Pharisees in Luke 5:32: "I came to call not the [self] righteous, but sinners to repentance," he declared (Luke 5:32).

FOUR—Redefining Lostness

9. Elisabeth Elliot, *These Strange Ashes* (Harper and Row, 1975), p.132.

10. Richard Lovelace, *The Dynamics of Spiritual Life* (Inter-Varsity, 1979), p. 212*ff.*

SIX—Redefining Hope

11. John Steinbeck, *East of Eden* (Viking, 1952), p. 3. John Knowles, *A Separate Peace* (Macmillan, 1959), p. 45. Both are cited in C. Plantinga, *Engaging God's World: A Christian Vision of Faith, Learning, and*

Living (Eerdmans, 2002), p. 3. My thinking on spiritual homesickness is indebted to Plantinga's whole first chapter.

12. C. S. Lewis, *The Weight of Glory and Other Addresses* (Simon and Schuster, 1996), pp. 28–29, 35–26.

SEVEN—The Feast of the Father

13. W. Kimnach, K. Minkema, D. Sweeney, eds, *The Sermons of Jonathan Edwards: A Reader* (Yale, 1999), pp. 127–128.

14. Martin Luther, *A Commentary on St. Paul's Epistle to the Galatians* (James Clarke, 1953), p. 101.

15. C. S. Lewis, *The Four Loves* (Harcourt, 1960), pp. 61–62.

About the Author

Timothy Keller was born and raised in Pennsylvania and educated at Bucknell University, Gordon-Conwell Theological Seminary, and Westminster Theological Seminary. He was first a pastor in Hopewell, Virginia. In 1989 he started Redeemer Presbyterian Church in Manhattan with his wife, Kathy, and their three sons. Today Redeemer has nearly six thousand regular attendees at five services, a host of daughter churches, and is planting churches in large cities throughout the world.